PERGAMON INSTITUTE OF ENGLISH
(OXFORD)

World Language English Series

ENGLISH FOR INTERNATIONAL
COMMUNICATION

Other titles of interest:

KRASHEN, Stephen
Second Language Acquisition and Second Language Learning

KRASHEN, Stephen
Principles and Practice in Second Language Acquisition

LEWIS, E. Glyn
Bilingualism and Bilingual Education

LOVEDAY, Leo
The Sociolinguistics of Learning and Using a Non-native Language

STREVENS, Peter
Teaching English as an International Language

TOSI, Arturo
Immigration and Bilingual Education

ENGLISH FOR INTERNATIONAL COMMUNICATION

Edited by

CHRISTOPHER BRUMFIT

University of London Institute of Education

PERGAMON PRESS

Oxford · New York · Toronto · Sydney · Paris · Frankfurt

U.K.	Pergamon Press Ltd., Headington Hill Hall, Oxford OX3 0BW, England
U.S.A.	Pergamon Press Inc., Maxwell House, Fairview Park, Elmsford, New York 10523, U.S.A.
CANADA	Pergamon Press Canada Ltd., Suite 104, 150 Consumers Rd., Willowdale, Ontario M2J 1P9, Canada
AUSTRALIA	Pergamon Press (Aust.) Pty. Ltd., P.O. Box 544, Potts Point, N.S.W. 2011, Australia
FRANCE	Pergamon Press SARL, 24 rue des Ecoles, 75240 Paris, Cedex 05, France
FEDERAL REPUBLIC OF GERMANY	Pergamon Press GmbH, 6242 Kronberg-Taunus, Hammerweg 6, Federal Republic of Germany

First edition 1982

Library of Congress Cataloguing in Publication Data
Main entry under title:
English for international communication
(World language English series)
Papers presented at a conference sponsored by the English-Speaking Union and held at Dartmouth House in London, in November 1980.
Contents: The English-Speaking Union's English language activities / H. D. Hicks—English as an international language I / Christopher Brumfit—English as an international language II / H. G. Widdowson—[etc.]
1. English language in foreign countries—Congresses.
2. English language—Study and teaching—Foreign students —Congresses. 3. Communication, International—Congresses.
I. Brumfit, Christopher. II. English-Speaking Union. III. Series.
PE2751.E55   1982   420'.9   81-21071   AACR2

British Library Cataloguing in Publication Data
English for international communication.—(World language English series)
1. English language—Usage—Congresses
I. Brumfit, Christopher II. Series
428.2'.4   PE1460
ISBN 0-08-028613-5

Printed in Great Britain by A. Wheaton & Co. Ltd., Exeter

PREFACE

BUCKINGHAM PALACE.

Co-operation depends on communication and this in turn depends on language. In the Middle Ages Latin provided a common language for the educated minority and later French took its place. In more recent times attempts have been made to create an artificial common language without much success.

Modern technical means of travel and communication have made the need for a language for international purposes a matter of considerable urgency. Indeed practical necessity has already resulted in the use of English in Air Traffic Control and in communications at sea world-wide. Furthermore, something like 600 million people use English as their first or second language already. Therefore in the absence of a truly international language it seems reasonable to investigate the possibilities of developing a language based on English as a means of international communication, primarily for special purposes such as science, engineering, commerce and other international activities.

It was to pursue these ideas that the English Speaking Union organised a conference last November on 'English for International Communication'. This brought together linguistic experts, teachers of English as a foreign language, and the users of English as an international language to discuss the problems and opportunities for further development. Many interesting and valuable papers were read at the meeting and I am delighted that Pergamon have agreed to publish them in this volume. I hope they will stimulate more interest in the subject and encourage further co-operation in the creation of a simple and practical language capable of meeting all the needs of specialist international communication.

1981

THE ENGLISH-SPEAKING UNION'S ENGLISH LANGUAGE ACTIVITIES

The initiative of Pergamon in publishing these papers is greatly welcomed, not only because of their intrinsic merit, but because the Conference at which they were given marks a significant step forward in the English language activities of the English-Speaking Union.

The English-Speaking Union was founded in 1918 to promote goodwill and understanding amongst English speaking peoples and apart from defining its areas of interest, the English language occupied little of its thoughts or activities at that time. These were concerned mainly with helping students to study and travel abroad through a wide variety of exchange schemes and scholarships and with arranging conferences, seminars and lectures. It was not until the 1970's that the English-Speaking Union, following the line that understanding depends upon communication, began to take a specific interest in the English language. An advisory Committee was formed and a *list of the members who cover different aspects of the language is shown below.

The first practical outcome, inspired by HRH The Duke of Edinburgh, was the English Language Competition, which was designed to stimulate new ideas in the field of learning and teaching English as a medium of international communication. The Competition was launched in 1977 on a national basis and from 1978 onwards was put on a world-wide basis. Each year entries of four to five thousand words are received from teachers and research workers all over the world. They are assessed by the English-Speaking Union's English Language Committee and also passed to publishers with the result that many of the ideas arising from the Competition have found a practical outlet through publishers of English language teaching materials.

Another project that was given birth at about the same time was the search for the number and kind of English words necessary for foreign scientists and technologists to communicate with each other assuming they had a common scientific or technological background. Thanks to sponsorship by Shell International, the English-Speaking Union, after pilot studies, was able to set up a

* C. J. Brumfit, C. N. Candlin, R. A. Close, A. Copisarow, A. C. Gimson, Dame Mary Green, J. Hambrook, J. Haycraft, H. D. Hicks, H. R. Howse, W. R. Lee, A. Macmillan, M. MacMillan, D. Y. Morgan, R. Quirk, P. D. Strevens, H. G. Widdowson, A. L. Williams.

programme of research at Cambridge University organized by Peter Nancarrow. The method was to convert Chinese scientific texts into "Semi-English" by computer, eliminate the scientific words leaving a residue of simple English linking words. The effectiveness of the "Semi-English" as a medium of scientific communication is still being tested at the Cavendish Laboratories in Cambridge. An interesting outcome of this basic work has been an improved capability to convert English back into Chinese and other languages and new research is being initiated to develop these techniques still further. The main difference between Nancarrow's approach and others is the emphasis on converting meaningful sections of text and not on word for word translation or syntax.

The growing interest of the English-Speaking Union in the English language resulting from the Competition and the Project led to the idea of a conference at which interested bodies from all over the world could attend or be represented. The idea became fact and the Conference took place at the end of November, 1980, in Dartmouth House; one hundred and four participants from places as far apart as Argentina, Australia, Japan, Nigeria, USA and a number of European countries attended. The scope, although within the overall theme of international communication, was very wide, and eighteen papers were read ranging from pure academic grammatical studies to practical business courses in English. Most of the participants have since indicated their support for further conferences with more specific terms of reference but designed to improve international communication and understanding through the use of the English language. The English-Speaking Union is grateful to Christopher Brumfit for producing this selection of papers from the Conference and writing a special introduction.

These are the three main lines of approach but the English-Speaking Union is also concerned with many other aspects of the English language including world-wide testing, simplification and linguistic aspects of literature and terminological data banks. New ideas are being considered and there is every reason to believe that these activities will become a permanent part of the English-Speaking Union's strategy to promote understanding throughout the world.

H. D. HICKS
Director of Education
English-Speaking Union

ACKNOWLEDGEMENTS

We are grateful to the following for permission to reproduce the material indicated:

Macmillan (London), for Quirk, *International Communication and the Concept of Nuclear English*.

CONTENTS

1. *Theoretical Problems*

ENGLISH AS AN INTERNATIONAL LANGUAGE I: WHAT DO WE MEAN BY "ENGLISH"?

CHRISTOPHER BRUMFIT

University of London Institute of Education

It is the purpose of this short preliminary paper to consider what kind of a claim we are making when we talk loosely about English as an international language. The phrase conceals a number of possible claims, and it is worthwhile for us to disentangle them as far as possible if we are to distinguish between different types of argument.

First of all it is quite clear that as a statement of simple fact English *is* an international language in that it is the most widespread medium of international communication, both because of the number and geographical spread of its speakers, and because of the large number of non-native speakers who use it for part at least of their international contact. The predominance of English is mainly the result of two periods of world domination by English speaking countries: British imperialism in the nineteenth century, and the economic influence of the United States in the twentieth century. The combination of political influence and technological superiority acquired through these two successive movements has given English an advantage over other major imperial languages such as French or Spanish, while the relative geographical restrictions of Russian, Chinese in its many forms or Arabic have made these languages less influential internationally. It should be noted, though, that this manifest international success has inevitably been bought at some cost. A language which can be identified with the largest nineteenth century imperial power or with the greatest capitalist power of the twentieth century will inevitably be perceived as an instrument of cultural and ideological domination in parts of the world where the language situation is unstable enough to demand debate. In many places, including India, many parts of Africa, France, Italy and Latin America, the role of English has come under strong attack within the last twenty years.

Yet we need to be clear what the choices are. There is a naive view of linguistic imperialism which argues that people have a right to be brought up in their own culture with their own language, and that outsiders should defend this right because of the evil effects of external domination. This view, which does have the virtue of recognizing the genuine threat implicit in external linguistic domination, nonetheless fails to recognize the complexity and power of the forces towards communication on a larger and larger scale. Isolation is impossible, and for many peoples the choice is between communication or exploitation. Possession of any language leads us to communicate with groups other than our own, and as the world becomes more and more interconnected by trade, improved communications, medical, political and cultural demands, the need for communication—as a way of enabling people to control and influence their own destinies—will inevitably increase. This will not necessarily lead to the emergence of *one* world language, but it must produce a demand for one or more auxiliary languages to complement those with only local currency. It is true that decisions about which languages should be promoted for national and international communication necessarily have to be sensitive to political, economic and ideological implications, but the only way in which contact with some major language can be avoided—for representatives of most groups of people in the world—is by remaining an isolated, ghettoized culture. Such a culture will either lose the benefits of wider economic and political contact altogether, or will be at the mercy of decisions made outside in which members of the minority group will have no voice.

It is often claimed, however, that in some sense English is peculiarly suited to be an international language. Such a claim may entail a number of different propositions, some of which follow from the present international status of English and some of which do not. It may be claimed, for example, that in some way the structure of English is peculiarly adapted for international communication, or that English is phonologically more accessible to most learners than other languages are. These are, it is true, questions of greater theoretical interest now than they were a few years ago. In linguistics it has normally been accepted as axiomatic that different languages are equally easy (or difficult) for native speakers to learn. However, it is important to recognize that this is a procedural axiom which is dependent on a view of all languages as developed and equally complex. A notion of differential competence among language users, which has become an increasingly interesting focus of investigation in the past decade, does allow us—at least in principle—to conceive of groups of language users whose language is relatively more simple than that of other groups. And further, if the acquisition of language is closely bound up with the uses to which it is put—that is, if the language structure acquired is a consequence of the functional load placed on it while it is being learnt—then a language responding to varied and diverse functional needs should in principle become in some sense richer than one which responds to a more limited set of functional demands. The increasing concern with language variation in recent years makes it possible to discuss such hypotheses without questioning the foundations on which descriptive linguistics rests.

But such discussion, while interesting to pursue, is still hypothetical. Nor do such arguments require that an internationally-used language should be more complex in structure than one used within one homogeneous culture. Functional variation and sensitivity may be achieved through increased vocabulary and an insistence on the public maintenance of fine distinctions of meaning. Any language is capable of enormous variation within its basic structure by the creation or borrowing of new words, and by a socially accepted concern for precision, rather than the tolerant vagueness of meaning characteristic of much casual speech. One language may be effective in far more spheres than another simply by virtue of a larger vocabulary and the social attitudes of its users. And it is social attitudes, also, which will influence the ease with which pronunciation can be learnt. There is probably more tolerance now of foreigner pronunciation than there was even a decade ago, as a result of our recognition that phonology is more negotiable than syntax in normal discourse. There seems to be little evidence that any language provides an overwhelming barrier phonologically if the social motivation for learning is provided by political or economic demands.

There are, however, two other types of claim which might be made for English. It might be claimed that the lexicon of English is peculiarly suited to international communication, or that it is in discourse terms well adjusted to the requirements of different cultures. Neither of these claims is especially interesting theoretically; indeed they may simply be tautological on the claim that English is used internationally. The vocabulary of a language will expand, infinitely in principle, depending on the demands which are made on it, and any language carries within it the capacity to be modified to the demands of particular types of discourse. English may have been fortunate in its past, from these points of view, but that implies no virtue for its future.

The same claim might be extended beyond the language to its users. It is a possibility that speakers of English are more tolerant of foreigner talk than speakers of some other languages. It may even be possible that such speakers are more tolerant of lexical innovation than others. But such characteristics cannot be attributed to the language itself: they are more likely to be features of a culture which may coincide to a large extent, but which cannot be co-extensive with speakers of the language. Only a strong Whorfian position would allow us to relate directly from language to users in this way. Anyway, it is perfectly possible to conceive of a political reaction to the overseas use of English which would lead to a much greater movement towards intolerance and a consequent restriction on native speaker acceptance of deviation. We might then wish to claim that the process of internationalization has gone too far to be halted, and that English is no longer the possession of native speakers, but this, again, is simply an inevitable consequence of the statement that English is *de facto* an international language.

So far it has been argued that claims about the suitability of English to be an international language on the grounds of its internal characteristics are consequences rather than causes of its international status; they are all in essence tautological. Another claim which could be made also reflects the accidental fact of its world dominance, but has more interesting repercussions for discussion of the future. We may concede that there is nothing intrinsic to English as a language which makes it qualified for international status, but still point to the widely attested fact of the world demand for the language as an illustration of the motivation to learn it, which makes it more likely that it can successfully achieve a firm international base and remain unrivalled. Certainly, the motivation to learn English exists, to the pleasure of teachers of English overseas—as with North Sea oil, from no merit of our own we find we are living on a rich commercial asset, providing we do not fritter it away by economic mismanagement—but it is a motivation which could of course disappear if the political and economic circumstances changed. The motivation is dependent on the learners' vision of themselves as members of a more-or-less English using culture, at least for some purposes, and a culture which is highly valued to justify the effort, time and money to be expended on learning English rather than doing more attractive things. Consequently, any discussion of the use of English for international purposes must eventually come to consider how to make teaching easier, quicker and cheaper. The large-scale motivation can only be a response to the larger historical movements which are outside individual control, but the other side of the equation can be confronted more directly, as many of the papers from the English Speaking Union Conference do.

Much discussion of teaching is essentially concerned with problems of simplification, an interest with a long and honourable pedigree in English language teaching. For many years vocabulary simplification and grading has been investigated and practised by learners and researchers in written materials and by teachers as they improvised in the classroom. More recent work, though possibly pedagogically less well-founded, has concentrated on structural simplification. And teachers through their classroom methodology have practised grading in discourse terms (and indeed phonologically) long before such procedures were described by linguists and classroom researchers. At the same time there have been a number of attempts to achieve simple systems for the learning of English (Basic English being perhaps the most famous) both within and without the formal educational systems. Throughout the past century there have been successions of successful "methods", usually combining simplification procedures, of variable sophistication, using methodological innovations and skilful marketing. Some of these have even been taken up by parliamentarians as answers to the perennial problems of language learning.

Discussion of simplification has often been confused, however, for there seem to be two separable issues at stake. Not everyone who wants to learn "English" is actually after a fully-fledged language, at least in the first instance. Many professions of communication need basic systems, which use English words and even basic English structure, to provide a simple and accessible code. Perhaps the languages of the sea, discussed at the conference, or of air traffic control, fit into this category. In many ways the use of English tokens for this limited use of language is fortuitous. Although the language used may allow very limited negotiation, it is not very different from the perfectly recited descriptions of exhibits at the Shanghai Trade Fair provided by Chinese guides who cannot answer a single question when asked. The characteristic of a language is not its formal features but its ability to be used for the negotiation of meaning. Some simple languages need to be only minimally negotiable (indeed they may prove literally disastrous if they are open to negotiation, as with air traffic controllers), but for this reason their relation with genuine language learning is slight. They are necessary, but they should not be confused with the languages which do require full human participation. To learn the latter requires at least three conditions to be fulfilled:

(a) there must be extensive exposure (some would say systematic exposure) to the target language;
(b) there must be extensive opportunity to use the language so far acquired as creatively as possible—through reading, writing, conversation, listening activities, whichever are most appropriate to particular learners;
(c) students must be motivated to benefit from (a) and (b).

It is unclear whether teachers can do very much about (c) except in a limited way by the efficiency and excitement of their work. But (a) and (b) are of course within the teacher's control. One of the issues which is by no means clearly resolved—and which is discussed in several papers here—is the nature of the exposure to the target language. There are those who argue that we should attempt to teach something which is a simplified version of English, that the target for the non-native speaker should be different from the native-speaker model. This claim can be interpreted in two ways. We may say as a matter of fact that non-native speakers do not become indistinguishable from native speakers so that we should recognize this in expecting them to attain simply to the standards of the best speakers from their linguistic group. (In practice this usually means being markedly deviant in accent, perhaps slightly deviant in spoken syntax, and scarcely deviant at all in writing except where cultural variation demands unEnglish forms in order to express a foreign culture.) This position, paradoxically, involves recognizing the non-native speaker as equivalent to the native, for native speakers too reveal their origins in accent, deviate in spoken syntax, and only vary in writing where there are significant cultural differences to express. The second interpretation is that we can specify a simpler form of English which is peculiarly suitable for international use. Here the crucial issue is whether we want the simple form to be learner created or teacher (or materials writer) dictated. There is plenty of evidence that learners create their own simple systems out of the English to which they are exposed, and that they fossilize at levels of attainment below those demanded by examinations or employers (though of course many learners continue to develop until they become indistinguishable from native speakers except in accent). Whether or not there is a strong case for de-

liberately creating a special language for students to learn presumably depends on the claims that such a language will in fact be easier to learn and
teach, and that such a language will be able to perform adequately in interaction with the English being produced in return—that it possesses the essential
negotiating capacity of a naturally usable language. Since it is difficult to imagine a situation where such a simple language will be used to converse solely
with other users of the simple language (for insofar as it is used naturally it
will expand naturally and will stop being simple). it is likely that the simple
language will eventually be required as a source for, at the very least, comprehension of natural English. In other words the simple language must in the
long run be seen as a pedagogic device in relation to learning normal English,
not as a substitute for normal English. The problems of creating a culture of
Basic English users, Esperanto users or of users of any other artificially
created language are insuperable. But the value of a language which assists
the process of language acquisition so that learners can exploit their own
capacities most effectively will be enormous.

At the same time, though, there will be a curious relationship between any
simple, pedagogical language and natural culture. The process of live language use which is increasingly being seen as necessary for language acquisition as well as language maintenance depends on the language, whether native or foreign, expressing a living culture. Consequently, while it is possible
to maintain that in principle the teaching of a language is teaching a tool for
use with no ideological or social implications, the successful take-up of this
teaching must depend on learners integrating the language with their own
ideological and social needs. The extent to which teachers need actively to assist this process has been a matter for debate for some time. It is true that, in
the context of highly specialized ESP groups, the cultural and social context
may be well defined in relation to particular technical and scientific needs, but
these nonetheless constitute a culture, and even ESP language work normally
spills over into wider concerns as soon as it is fully taken over by students, for
it is rare for language users to achieve total separation between the various
social roles that they play. The stronger the movement towards a functional
view of language teaching, the greater the necessity for it to be seen as coordi-
nated with the social, political, economic, even ethical and religious needs of
learners.

All this leads to a curious paradox. There is a strong movement throughout
the world towards greater communication across cultures, and the English
language cannot avoid having a major role to play in this process. This is a
sociological fact. But there are risks as well as advantages in this process for
the native-speaking English countries. On the one hand we shall benefit culturally in many ways by having direct access to cultures which are historically
and geographically far away from ourselves, as English is used for secondary
purposes by more and more people outside our traditional spheres of influence. And we shall no doubt achieve economic, even perhaps some political
advantages, by sharing a common language. But we risk also creating em-

nities as well as loyalties. There is already evidence that the varied sources of English are being exploited by countries in their attitudes to learning English. American English may be preferred to British by countries wishing to express their independence from a traditional British connection; countries too closely connected by geography or history to the States have been known to turn towards Britain for a change in model and teaching policy for their English. Perhaps the same is happening in contacts with Australia or New Zealand. The English-Speaking world can be played politically by the non-English-Speaking world. Nor need this process be seen solely between the varieties of the English language. At the beginning of this paper it was argued that the world must have international languages—but there is no necessity for there to be only one. People, and nations, need to be able to hide behind misunderstanding as well as reveal all to each other. The world, unless it manifests an unprecedented desire for unity in the near future, will require a minimum of two international languages, if only to play them off against each other in self-defence. The paradox for the development of English as an international language is that the more multicultured English becomes, the more it will be perceived as a threat and the more it will, in the end, lead people to wish for some alternatives to English. In the meantime, however, users of the English language have been provided with a unique opportunity for cross-cultural contact on a hitherto unprecedented scale. The immediate gains will be not merely political and economic, but linguistic and pedagogic also, as we understand more fully the process of linguistic adaptation to the widely varied needs of people throughout the world.

ENGLISH AS AN INTERNATIONAL LANGUAGE II: WHAT DO WE MEAN BY "INTERNATIONAL LANGUAGE"?

H. G. WIDDOWSON

University of London Institute of Education

I do not think that we can be clear about the issues relating to the use of English as an international language without invoking questions of much wider import about the nature of human behaviour in general. Language is so intricately bound up with everything we do and everything we are that any attempt to extract it for common utilitarian purposes will require the most cautious surgery. What I want to do in this brief contribution is to indicate the complexity of the extraction problem and to suggest that its very nature may well preclude a satisfactory solution.

There is, in very general terms, a fundamental opposition in all human affairs between two forces. One of these impels us towards exploration and the establishment of wider networks of communication. The other directs us to a consolidation of our own domain and a preservation of our particular identity. These forces, functions of the homing and questing instincts respectively, appear in various guises in myth and folk tale. One son stays at home to tend the family fields, the other sets out to seek his fortune. They are at work too in the ordinary business of everyday life where we are faced with the continuing task of reconciling these contraries.

Language quite naturally reflects these forces and affords us the means of achieving a reconciliation between them. When we use it to make contact with others and to engage in the negotiation of meaning we subscribe to what has been referred to as the co-operative principle. This requires us to advance into the domain of the other person while at the same time allowing him reciprocal access to our own. Engagement in communicative activity thus entails encroachment on the one hand and exposure on the other. It is a risky business. Of course, where the domains of the interlocutors are already in close convergence as a consequence of shared knowledge and experience, the risk is reduced. Communication between members within the same tightly knit social network will obviously not create the same tension as communication between strangers, since there will be an extensive overlap of domain. It is where domains are distinct and at some distance from each other that difficulties arise.

So co-operation, though necessary to social life, can involve considerable risk to the individual's security. When the risk seems greater than the benefits of co-operation, the individual retires to the safety of his own familiar world. There are times when such retirement becomes permanent, when the individual withdraws entirely from external engagement and remains enclosed within his own seclusion. Most of us, however, have need of continuing involvement and have to face up to the problem of calculating the risks on every occasion of social contact.

On the one hand then there is the co-operative imperative: an extrovert and exploratory force. On the other hand, there is the territorial imperative: an introvert force, which acts in the interests of personal security. Language has the resources to service both imperatives: it enables us to be explicit about our intended messages and to be protective of self-esteem as well.

An example: if I wish to convey to somebody my desire that he should carry out a certain action, say, that of lending me £10, then the English language will provide me with the means of conveying my message in the most directly accessible way:

Lend me ten pounds.

It is unlikely, however, that I would broach such a subject so abruptly outside the circle of my closest intimates since to do so would run a serious risk of rebuff. So, I would be disposed to proceed more protectively:

I am sorry to bother you but I wonder if I might ask you a favour . . .

Such an approach allows for disengagement if danger threatens. It also, of course, protects my interlocutor from the embarrassment of a direct refusal. On both sides face is preserved and there has been no trespass on personal territory.

Every use of language, then, represents a reconciliation of these opposing forces. There will be times, obviously, when the need for co-operative action is so urgent that the claims of territorial respect are held in abeyance. There are situations, too, when one of the interlocutors is not thought to be deserving of any territorial respect at all. These conditions call for language use which is so explicit as to leave no room for protective features. On other occasions, it will be these protective features which have to predominate, when we need to be defensive and wary.

I have spoken of the way language is used to protect the domain of the individual's life-space. But, of course, language is used to create this domain as well in the process of socialization. The individual finds his essential security in the membership of groups who share his conception of the world, who subscribe to the same cultural values. Language is used not only to convey this communal reality, but also to represent it: it is not only used to communicate what members of social groups mean but also to indicate what it means to be a member of a social group. It can be directly expressive of the sense of belonging.

So it is that different groups of speakers develop their own way of speaking, not only to achieve a more exact reference to the world they share but also to express their group identity. Language in this latter identifying function is a sign of solidarity, and marks the enclosure of territory. In this respect, it is directed *against* co-operation and towards self-containment. One obvious example of this is what we call slang: a way of speaking deliberately designed to establish group solidarity, to exclude strangers, and to preclude its use as a means of co-operation between different groups. Indeed, when slang terms do take on wider currency they tend to be replaced by others so that their exclusiveness as insignia is preserved.

It is, then, of the very nature of human language that is serves the *communicative* function of providing for the conveyance of meanings between social groups and the *identifying* function of expressing and preserving intra-group identity. The first of these can be seen as a realization of the co-operative imperative and the second as a realization of the territorial imperative. The more effective a particular language is as the expression of an area of communal knowledge and experience constituting the shared domain of a group, the easier it will be to communicate within the group and the more difficult it will be to use that language for inter-group communication. In this sense, then, identifying and communicative functions are in opposition; and their opposition results in the somewhat paradoxical consequence that we can communicate most easily with those whom we have least need to communicate with.

What bearing does this have on the role, actual or potential, of English as an international language? When people refer to this, they are, I would suppose, not usually thinking of English as a common identifying expression of universal norms of thought and experience. At least, I would hope that they are not, though one can never be quite sure. There are, no doubt, still some fundamentalist visionaries about who interpret the brotherhood of man quite literally as a realizable ideal and who see all societies as constituents of one vast and homogeneous social group with English as their means of identification, all subscribing to the same set of beliefs, all recognizing the same canons of acceptable behaviour. It is a dangerous ideal. Such visions have generally been associated in the past with the imposition of ideologies of one sort or another, the winning over of hearts and minds, the saving of souls. This has left its legacy of distrust. The worry about linguistic imperialism derives from a recognition of the identifying power of language, which can dominate cultural domains and invest them with an alien order of reality.

Is it possible, then, to conceive of English, or any natural language, operating only as a common communicative amenity, as an entirely neutral medium for the conveyance of information? This is what many people seem to have in mind when they talk of English as an international language. But there are dangers here too. A language stripped down to its bare essentials as a resource for impersonal reference is deprived at the same time of its potential for creativity and change, and the humanity of its users is diminished accordingly. 1984 is now close upon us: the age of Newspeak:

> "It's a beautiful thing, the destruction of words. Of course the great wastage is in the verbs and adjectives, but there are hundreds of nouns that can be got rid of as well. It isn't only the synonyms; there are also the antonyms. After all, what justification is there for a word which is simply the opposite of some other word? A word contains its opposite in itself. Take 'good' for instance. If you have a work like 'good', what need is there for a word like 'bad'? 'Ungood' will do just as well—better, because it's an exact opposite, which the other is not. Or, again, if you want a stronger version of 'good', what sense is there in having a whole string of vague useless words like 'excellent' and 'splendid' and all the rest of them? 'Plusgood' covers the meaning; or 'doubleplusgood' if you want something stronger still. Of course we use those forms already, but in the final version of Newspeak there'll be nothing else. In the end the whole notion of goodness and badness will be covered by only six words—in reality, only one word."

> (George Orwell, 1984)

This kind of reduction (and there are counterparts in fact to Orwell's fiction) will result in increased referential efficiency so long as the frame of reference is fixed. Such a reduction, if maintained, will itself establish the conditions for fixity as all new experience will have to be cramped into the only code available for expressing it. But as a language becomes, in this way, a self-signalling system which has no need of human agency, except as a means of transmission, it ceases to function as a natural language. As soon as the human factor intrudes, the language grows, changes, varies, becomes subject to the identifying need of speakers to express their own identity.

It seems to me that one is bound to be involved in serious difficulties, both practical and ethical, when one contrives to promote English as an international language, whether this is done by trying to conserve a common identifying integrity in the language or by trying to reconstruct it so that it improves in communicative efficiency.

But why, it might be asked, is promotion necessary anyway? English is already widely used throughout the world in these fields of academic and occupational endeavour which require a common means of communication between divergent social groups. So why not sustain this development rather than seek to direct it by intervention? It would seem to be more sensible to support the role that English has already acquired rather than to spend time and effort in dreaming up ways of making it more international than it already is.

Apart from the negative reason that such a course of action would avoid the difficulties I have mentioned, there are also good positive reasons for supporting existing uses of English for academic and occupational purposes. These uses represent varieties of English which have evolved to service the needs of groups whose members share specialist domains of knowledge and experience which are to a considerable extent dissociated from the values of primary culture expressed through the mother tongue. People like engineers, doctors, scientists, airline pilots and businessmen, whatever primary cultural values they subscribe to, acquire the secondary culture of their specialities and thereby take out membership of different occupational and professional groups without being involved in any conflict of loyalty. These groups quite naturally develop uses of English which give identity to their particular specialist domain and at the same time fulfil the necessary conditions for communicative efficiency.

The principal reason why English is an international language is because, by historical accident, it was found to be a convenient means for establishing international groups of people with purposes and expertise in common. The best service we can offer the world, it seems to me, is to support the use of English in this role by developing more effective ways of teaching it as it is. This might indeed involve some deliberate reduction of linguistic complexity, but only as a transitional measure, justified by pedagogic principle, to facilitate the language learning process; not as a means of refashioning the language itself. Any refashioning of the language necessary to maintain its communicative efficiency and identifying integrity can be left, as it always has been, to the agency of the users themselves as they adjust it quite naturally to meet changing needs and circumstances.

INTERNATIONAL COMMUNICATION AND THE CONCEPT OF NUCLEAR ENGLISH

RANDOLPH QUIRK

University College, London

International communication—an indisputable desideratum—does not presuppose, let alone prescribe, a single international language. But it has long been held as virtually axiomatic that this would constitute the ideal basis. For over a century,[1] and especially in the past quarter-century, we have come to believe that this goal is within reach, with English rating a greater world spread than any other language in recorded history. Yet within the past decade, many people have started to wonder: people concerned with international affairs in general as well as members of the profession engaged throughout the world in teaching English.

The doubts have been arising on two grounds:

(a) the degree of variation in the forms of English in use—fears, indeed, of its rapid dissolution; and

(b) the practicability—not least in view of (a)—of teaching the language, especially on a mass scale, to the level required for international usefulness, given the enormous deployment of educational resources that this demands.

The divergence between one man's English and another's is great enough to be striking (though hardly, I think, alarming) within each of the English-Speaking countries. The steadfast Anglo-Saxon opposition to academy-style attempts at standardization has harmonized in recent years with an educationist's orthodoxy discouraging interference with a child's most local and intimately felt language. The absurdities of an earlier generation's preoccupation with "correctness" have been abandoned, and in some places the pendulum has swung to a position where quite extreme permissiveness has been actually encouraged. Where this trend has coincided with political movements towards community identity (as with "Black English" in the United States), counter-standard policies have become especially radical without anyone—so it seems to me—having much clear perception of the long-term implications.

15

Naturally, in this context, the divergence between one country's English and another's is seen to be in danger of growing much more seriously wide, with no common educational or communicational policy even theoretically applicable, but rather with nationalism strongly (if haphazardly and even unconsciously) endorsing a linguistic independence to match political and other aspects of independence. The voices of Australia and New Zealand and the Irish Republic (as heard for instance on the national radio) are as limited to purely intranational norms as are those of Britain and the United States. I shall say something later of centripetal influences, not least in the name "English" being applied confidently to all these varieties. But it would be idle to pretend that the name itself is adequate guarantee of linguistic integrity or that the varieties of English used in Britain, America and Australia are more unified than the varieties of "Scandinavian" used in Norway, Sweden and Denmark where each is regarded—and named—as a separate language.[2]

Diversity within English is liable to be much greater, however, and to lead to far more acute problems in those countries (such as India, Nigeria, the Philippines) where English is not a native language but where it nevertheless has widespread use for administrative, commercial and other internal purposes. Here, in contrast to the native English-speaking countries where the language—in whatever variety—is naturally acquired, English has to be formally taught; and here therefore the question of standards is actively and often agonizingly debated. Since the teaching has to be done by teachers who had similarly to be taught the language and who inevitably learnt it to varying degrees of adequacy, change in the acceptable standards of achievement is not surprisingly very rapid. In any case, in a vast country like India, with a long history of English for internal communication, the natural processes of language–culture interaction have produced a large number of phonological, grammatical, lexical and stylistic features that have become thoroughly imbued and arguably inalienable (cf. Kachru, 1976). Indeed, with an estimated 25 million people making regular use of the language, India is the third largest country in the world with English established as a medium for internal purposes.

It is from this that there springs (by the imperfect analogy with British English, American English, and the like) the concept of recognizing Indian English as a comparable national variety with its own internal determinants of acceptability, however much it may be seen historically as largely derived from British English (cf. Strevens, 1977: 133, 140). Clearly, the range of English in India (from the pidginized dock-worker to the government clerk, to the judge, to the voice of All-India Radio) is very much greater than the nearest analogy in Britain or America—as well as sharply different in kind. Clifford Prator[3] is prominent among those who have argued that it is fundamentally unsound to encourage the recognition of non-native varieties of English. But so far as the subcontinent is concerned, the insightful researches of such specialized observers as Braj Kachru leave me convinced that it is not a matter of heresy but of accepting plain facts.[4]

Yet the facts are unquestionably daunting. We are confronted in the world by three, largely independent (and largely uncontrolled, if not uncontrollable), potentially limitless types of diversification within English. If we concede, with current educational orthodoxy, that the individual benefits by seeking community identity through repose in his most local variety of language, can we afford to neglect the same individual's needs in a wider role—ultimately as a "citizen of the world"? And what can be done, in this connection, to mitigate the growing despair of the teacher with day-to-day classroom concerns— not least in the English-speaking countries themselves, but of course far more acutely in countries teaching English as a foreign language and (with the present world's demands) on a mass scale?

Teaching any single one of the national varieties (say "standard southern British" English) is a hard enough assignment. With its gargantuan vocabulary, its subtly difficult syntax, and with the recently accentuated emphasis on teaching phonetic accuracy in speech, the language is difficult enough for a specially trained native speaker to teach with small classes of highly motivated pupils. But in the vast majority of classrooms all over the world, the teacher is not a native, his English is far from perfect, his training has been seriously inadequate, his classes are by no means small, and—partly as a result of all these factors—his pupils have by no means an automatically high motivation. Add to this an examining system that is seriously at variance with classroom goals and we clearly have a potentially disastrous situation even before we grapple with the fact that the initial postulate is in doubt. Can the teacher's model be "any single one of the national varieties"? And if so, which? And what guarantees can he (or his education authority) have of the international acceptability of that variety, now, or in fifteen years? Is the colossal allocation of national resources to the teaching of English worthwhile?

Now of course all this is to take a very black look at the black side of things. Such pessimism may be quite unjustified. Developing countries may get richer and be glad to maintain or even increase their contribution of GNP to teaching English. Better provision may be made for teacher training. Better methods of teaching English already in existence may be more widely implemented, and still better methods may yet be devised. We now have better dictionaries and grammars of English than we have ever had, and we are developing techniques for sensitizing learners to national and stylistic varieties of English and for helping them meet a predicted range of communicative needs. We are beginning to think more realistically of the goals in language learning and especially about whether it is reasonable or even responsible to seek achievement in a foreign language of all the skills we master more or less effortlessly in our native language.

Again, the diversity of English in the world may not in fact be leading to dissolution into several distinct languages. I am among many observers on record as seeing powerful centripetal, unifying forces at work, offsetting the fissiparous tendencies that local needs and nationalist susceptibilities are fostering (cf., for example, Quirk, 1972, 1978). Thanks in no small measure to a traditional spelling system which ignores the passing of the years as it transcends the vagaries of pronunciation, books and newspapers use a virtually identical English whether they originate in Bloomsbury or Baltimore, Canberra or Calcutta.[5]

As regards the spoken language, too, we must not ignore the impact of radio, television, film, faster travel, and even the wide access to the same pop songs. These factors are certainly making the different varieties familiar and comprehensible to increasingly large numbers of people, and to an observable degree as between British and American English at least, they seem to be causing productive usage to limit its variation.

But let us stay with the black side—not in any spirit of alarmist masochism but to look prudently for alternative strategies if our worst fears prove to be well-founded. What happens to English in the world (or—in due succession to English—any other language of international currency) if teaching the full language proves too costly, if new techniques of teaching turn out to be disappointing, if the natural process of language diversification effectively shatters the linguistic goal? Do we then abandon hopes for the universality of English? Do we switch to some other language in which there is less inhibition about proclaiming a single world standard? Do we abandon the democratic ideal of teaching English on a mass scale and swing instead to educating an elite small enough to make the teaching effective? Or do we abandon the idea of an international language altogether and contemplate a future of linguistic frontiers manned by faceless simultaneous translators?

It is in this context that some of us have been taking a fresh look at what linguistic theory may be able to provide. Now of course linguistics has been much involved in the turns and twists of language description and language teaching for a couple of generations, and many look upon its contributions with something less than enthusiastic gratitude. Many indeed attribute a large part of current disillusion to the intervention over the years by successive waves of brash "experts", at one and the same time advocating doctrinaire rigour in various fashionable methodologies and squishy permissiveness in goals, norms and standards. But we need not throw away the bath water because we do not think the babies' faces are shining. Part of our trouble is that linguistics and the social sciences in general have remained at the data-gathering, model-building and speculative stage comparable to that of physics in the eighteenth century. In part also, no doubt, the emphasis in the current climate of opinion on environmental and cultural conservation is inhibiting our getting to the manipulating stage—manipulating the medium, that is (e.g. through planned simplification[6]), rather than only the learner. No doubt we have been rightly apprehensive of the danger of filling our green valleys with dark satanic linguistic mills. But it seems to me that the time has come to enquire whether linguistics and its sister disciplines are now mature enough to direct their insights not only to language description as hitherto but also to something more like language design.

For the purposes of this enquiry, let me ask that the following propositions be regarded as axiomatic:

(1) The world needs a single medium for international communication ("needs" is important and implies willingness to pay the price—educational, social, cultural, even financial).

(2) The possibility of a wholly new or artificially constructed "language" has been excluded.[7]

(3) The only viable possibility is either (a) to adopt or (b) to adapt one of the world's natural languages: the starting point must be a linguistic force with existing momentum.

(4) The best current candidate for (3) is English. Bearing in mind the black picture I have seen fit to paint, however, one further assumption is required, namely that (3a) has been tried with dismal results and prospects. I thus postulate a situation in which we are left with (3b), and I would like to explore some of the questions that would be involved in adapting English (or of course any other language) to constitute a nuclear medium for international use.

To satisfy the relevant need, "Nuclear English" would have to possess certain general properties. It must be:

(a) decidedly easier and faster to learn than any variety of natural "full" English;

(b) communicatively adequate, and hence a satisfactory end-product of an educational system; and

(c) amenable to extension in the course of further learning, if and as required.

Communicative adequacy is to be understood as providing the learner with the means of expressing, however periphrastically, an indefinitely large number of communicative needs (in principle, all), with the minimum of ambiguity, the limit being imposed by his personal concerns and his intellectual capacity and not by the capacity of the medium. As to (c), extensibility may be thought of in terms of "English for Specific Purposes" modules—which would thus entail the property (independently required in any case) of the lexical and grammatical content being fully explicit, so that the "fit" of additional modules may be exactly predicted. But extensibility should also be seen in terms of less programmed skill-acquisition towards fully natural English in any major national variety, and this in turn entails that, since nothing should have to be "unlearned", the lexical and grammatical properties of Nuclear English must be a subset of the properties of natural English (presumably of the "common core", in the sense of Quirk *et al.*, 1972:1.15).

Both (b) and (c) are obviously vital in their own right. But they are vital also in anticipating misunderstandings about the nature and role of Nuclear English.

Culture-free as calculus, with no literary, aesthetic, or emotional aspirations, it is correspondingly more free than the "national Englishes" of any suspicion that it smacks of linguistic imperialism or even (since native speakers of English would also have to be trained to use it) that it puts some countries at an advantage over others in international communication. Since it is not (but is merely related to) a natural language, it would not be in competition for educational resources with foreign languages proper but rather with that other fundamental interdisciplinary subject, mathematics. Nor, by the same token, could its teachers be accused of wasting resources (as sometimes happens, distressingly, with foreign languages and literatures) on an elitist disciplinary ornament for the few. The relations of Nuclear English are less with the ivory tower than the public convenience.

Equally, however, (b) and (c) make clear that Nuclear English can carry no such stigma as that frequently perceived (however unjustly) in relation to basilect forms of English or the pidgins of tropical seaports. It is not a matter of offering a second-class language to the masses of the twenty-first century where the elite of the nineteenth and twentieth were privileged to have English in all its storied splendour, metaphysicals and all. The emblematic consumers of Nuclear English should not be seen as Indonesian children in a village school room, but as Italian and Japanese company directors engaged in negotiating an agreement.

Reluctantly ignoring issues in the lexicon,[8] let me ponder a little on seeking appropriate nuclei in grammar. It might, for example, be decided that the English tag question (so often in the English of Wales and Southeast Asia replaced by the invariant *isn't it?*) was disproportionately burdensome, with its requirements of reversed polarity, supply of tensed operator and congruent subject:

> I'm late, aren't I? am I not?
> She used to work here, didn't she?
> They oughtn't to go there, ought they?

For all of the italicized pieces, whose function as a response promotor is arguably worth retaining, we could achieve the same objective with *isn't that right?* or *is that so?*, in full English a perfectly acceptable expression though of course a minority one (except as shortened to "right" in AmE).

Or again, there is arguably no need for non-restrictive relative clauses, many of which are in any case semantically inexplicit:

> I chatted with the captain, who was later reprimanded.
> I expressed my sympathy to the captain, who had been reprimanded.

If these mean, respectively,

> I spoke to the captain and as a result he was (later) reprimanded.
> I expressed my sympathy to the captain because he had been reprimanded.

it would do no harm to say so and at the same time rid us of structures that could be misunderstood (especially in writing) as restrictive clauses. Nor need we retain in Nuclear English the option to construct noun clauses or restrictive relative clauses with "zero" particle ("He was afraid she was hurt", "The man she loves"), and with non-restrictive clauses gone we could generalize that as the single invariant particle for relative and noun clauses.

A further example: we need non-finite constructions with certain verbs like *cause* which will almost certainly (unlike perhaps *condescend* and *assist*) remain in the nuclear lexicon: "He caused the experiment to fail". But we could exclude this construction where it was merely optional for a that-clause and hence banish the multiple ambiguous "They expected a doctor to examine John" (the more readily so if, in addition, the lexicon admitted *expect* in only one of the conventional senses).

In none of these instances, it will be noticed, does the "solution" lie in going beyond the rules of ordinary acceptable English. But equally noteworthy: nor has the proposed solution any bearing at all upon frequency of occurrence in ordinary English. If anything (as we shall see below with modal auxiliaries), the most frequent items are those that are most likely to be excluded from Nuclear English since they are the most polysemous. Rather, the solution must lie in a principled mediation between (a) the grammatical structure of ordinary English and (b) a language-neutral assessment of communicative needs. The order here is vital: the starting point must be (a), not (b). If we adopted the converse, we might for example seek a number system going beyond the existing two terms ("singular" and "plural") to include a third ("dual") in view of the large number of items in human experience that go in two's (eyes, thumbs, feet, parents, etc.). An additional inflection (parent sg, parenten dual, parents pl) would enable us to avoid the ambiguity that is common in sentences like:

The permission of parents is required.

(Does each child need to get permission from both parents or will the permission of only one be sufficient?) Needless to say, such a proposal would infringe one of the basic properties of Nuclear English (that it should contain nothing that had to be "unlearned" by the user who proceeded to any extension beyond it) and would therefore be rejected.

The starting point must therefore remain firmly in the grammar of ordinary English, and the major systems (like countability, transitivity, gender, tense) will be retained along with their ordinary exponents, their use defined explicitly in terms of relevant communicative needs. By "major systems" would be understood those affecting more than one word-class and having reverberations on other systems—as in the case of the count/non-count distinction which is reflected in both the determiner system and in verb inflection.

Much research and experiment will be necessary to find out the extent to which these principles can be translated into a blueprint for prescribing the grammar of Nuclear English. Unquestionably, there will be many problems in identifying for omission those minor systems for which alternative expression can be found within major ones. Thus (in terms of Quirk *et al.*, 1972) "complex transitive" and "di-transitive" structures might reasonably be excised from the transitivity system. We glimpsed a possible treatment of complex transitives in the *expect* example above. Ditransitives are on the face of it even easier to handle—through replacement by the corresponding prepositional alternative:

We offered the girl a drink.
We offered a drink to the girl.

But there is the problem of certain verbs for which there is no prepositional alternative (cf. "He charged her a high rent") and of verbs on the other hand which have alternative prepositional complementation (cf. "serve X to Y" = "serve Y with X"). It is of course likely that verbs with such lexical compression would be replaced by nuclear periphrases ("He caused her to pay a high rent", "He said that it was necessary that she pay . . ."), but to the extent that such verbs are retained in the lexicon on purely lexicological grounds, they present interesting difficulties as to grammatical treatment.

More miscellanea of this kind could be easily supplied, but I shall confine my attention to the problems posed by the modals, an area of notorious difficulty in English and other languages, and liable to cause difficulty in communication even between native speakers. I shall begin with a reminder of the complexities, and in the course of what follows I shall attempt to project what must be conveyed in Nuclear English

Take one of those doom-laden stellar conjunctions beloved of Arthur Hailey. We're in an electric storm over Indiana on a flight from New York (herafter designated—quite fictitiously, needless to say—Able Baker 123). In the bad and intermittent radio reception, our pilot hears a ground control voice:

Able Baker 123 may land at O'Hare in five minutes.

Now, it is easy for the philosopher or linguist in his study to see that this is ambiguous. But for the ordinary speaker in discourse, including the ordinary pilot on the flight deck, speech contains no ambiguities: we tune in to the meaning that happens to be uppermost in our expectations. If the pilot thinks he is merely eavesdropping on a message about his aircraft to someone else, he will at once interpret it as:

Able Baker 123 will possibly land at O'Hare in five minutes.

an expression of opinion which he will check against the probabilities suggested by other factors, including his instruments. If on the other hand he takes it to be a message addressed to himself, he will just as instantaneously interpret it as:

Able Baker 123 is permitted to land at O'Hare in five minutes.

—a very different matter indeed. Either way, radio conditions may make it difficult to check or correct the interpretation.

If the radioed sentence used *can* and referred to an airfield not on his flight plan (say, Fort Wayne, Indiana), further possibilities occur, again without warning the hearer of their existence:

Able Baker 123 can land at Fort Wayne.

This could still mean "is permitted to land", but it might equally mean "has the capability of landing" (i.e. can adopt the right approach angle or has the appropriate landing speed for Fort Wayne; or Fort Wayne has a sufficiently long runway for a 747, or whatever). Then again, interpreted as a message between two controllers, the sentence could be interpreted as:

It is conceivable that we could divert Able Baker 123 to Fort Wayne.

Introduce a past marking and new ambiguities appear:

Able Baker 123 could have landed at Fort Wayne.

(=either "had the capability of landing . . . but didn't"; or "had the possibility . . . but didn't"; or "had permission to land . . . but didn't"; or even "It is possible that 123 did in fact land").

Withdrawing from air travel melodrama, we find analogous ambiguities with other modal expressions:

They ought to be here.

can mean "There was a requirement that they be here"; or "I expected that they were here, but they're not".

John WILL fail his exams!

can mean "I confidently predict that he will"; or "John persists in failing"; or even "I insist on his failing".

John must stay at home on Wednesdays

can mean "John is obliged to stay at home" or "It seems certain that John stays at home."

John is supposed to be asleep

can mean "There is a requirement on John to be asleep"; or "There is a requirement on us to believe that John is asleep"; or "People suppose that John is asleep".

Not surprisingly, as every EFL teacher knows, errors among foreign learners are legion and apparently ineradicable.[9] Even non-natives in post as university professors of English (let alone professionals in other disciplines, whatever their fluency) make errors like the following; indeed I have taken them from such sources:

You could like to forward the book to me	(for *might*)
For this reason he would not write it	(for *would not be writing*)
The study should be of great value	(for *would*)
The conductor arrived and the concert should start	(for *was due to*)
After many attempts, he could succeed	(for *was able to*)
The students had better write clearly	(for *should*)
He tells me that he must write it last year	(for *had to*)

There are additional difficulties lurking in the relation between assertive and non-assertive modality. Thus, although with some modals the correspondence is straightforward ("he can drive a car", He can't . . . / If he can . . . / Can he . . .?), with others it is not, and quite experienced non-natives are apt to slip into expressions like:

He must not complete his thesis before January
He may not answer every question

where "need not, is permitted not to" happens to be meant in both cases. And among the further difficulties, there are those arising from differences in discourse orientation: the contrasting expectations involved between for example *He may go* (which will probably be deontic but may be epistemic) and *I may go* (which will almost certainly be epistemic but may be deontic). (Cf. Palmer, 1974: 100ff.)

The problems inherent in modality have of course been the subject of discussion. In that pioneer study of linguistic engineering, the Essay Towards a Real Character of 1668, John Wilkins distinguished "primary" and "secondary modes", the latter being concerned in "modal propositions" where "the Matter in discourse . . . is concerned not simply by itself, but gradually in its causes" (p. 316). These modal propositions he sees as involving either contingency or necessity, each being itself bipartite. So far as contingency is concerned, either the speaker expresses "only the Possibility" of something (which is dependent "upon the power of its cause"), or "his own Liberty to it" (when there is "a freedom from all Obstacles either within or without"). With necessity, says Wilkins, "the speaker expresseth the resolution of his own will" or "some external obligation, whether Natural or Moral". As we could expect from this, when Wilkins comes subsequently to propose his "real characters", he offers distinct symbols for each of these modal values (p. 391).

It seems clear that Nuclear English cannot afford to do less. Whether we need more distinctions is quite another question. It will be noticed that Wilkins anticipates modern philosophers and linguists in his insistence on awareness of the speaker's involvement, but I am doubtful whether we need to follow more recent scholars in recognizing—at any rate explicitly—a three-tier modality in every sentence (designated neustic, tropic, and phrastic in Hare,

1970). But in view of the unfortunate overlaps demonstrable in the ordinary English use of modals, it seems clear that such factors bearing upon propositional content as the speaker's commitment, the factuality, and the constraint upon the agent need to be given formal expression.

Within speaker's commitment, we need further to bear in mind the relevant contrasts arising as between his knowledge, his belief, his desire, and his mere declaration. Factuality involves the range from certainty through probability to possibility and improbability. With constraints upon the agent, it is important to distinguish on the one hand between those that are internal to the agent (whether relating to his ability or to his volition) and those that are external to him (whether compulsion or absolute necessity on the one hand, or social or moral duty on the other).

These parameters enjoin the recognition of three theoretically quite distinct types of modality. We have epistemic modality expressing the degree of speaker's knowledge (e.g. He may go = "I think it possible that he will"); deontic or "root" modality expressing constraint, whether imposed by the speaker (as in imperatives) or by some other agency (such as the law); and potential modality, concerned with the agent's volition or ability. A fourth modality, alethic (cf. Lyons, 1977), can be disregarded in ordinary linguistic communication, concerned as it is with purely logical necessity ("Since he is unmarried, he must be a bachelor").

The question now arises as to how these modalities and their partially overlapping concerns with speaker, agent, and external world might best be expressed in Nuclear English. We might consider three possibilities.

(a) We could try to separate off those that are in some sense most "important"[10] and disregard the rest. This seems in effect to be what happens in pidgin languages such as Neo-Melanesian, but among its objectionable aspects would be the failure thereby to meet the requirement that Nuclear English must provide full communicative adequacy.

(b) We could retain the ordinary range of English modals but restrict their use to avoid overlap. Thus *may* might be restricted to epistemic use ("be possible") and excluded from deontic use ("be permitted"). This proposal has several disadvantages. It would tend not to oblige the speaker to analyse the precise intention of his message, and it would be very difficult for the speaker with a partial or good knowledge of "full" English to avoid making "mistakes" and forming just such ambiguous sentences as were illustrated earlier.

(c) We would retain the full range of modalities but restrict their expression to carefully prescribed and maximally explicit paraphrases,[11] banning the use of the normal modal auxiliaries altogether. This is a sharply radical proposal but it is of course in line with the theory of Nuclear English as envisaged in this paper. In repudiating the claims of "frequency in occurrence", we would achieve the objective of avoiding the ultimately far greater disadvantages of extreme polysemy. In requiring paraphrase, we would be insisting on a speaker's clarifying his own intention in advance, while yet expressing himself without departure from fully acceptable forms of ordinary English. Indeed, paraphrases of the kind "It is possible that this is not true", "It is not possible that this is true" present the means not only of separating modality from proposition but of stipulating such features as the scope of negation, frequently obscured in ordinary language. In all of which, we achieve a mode of expression reflecting distinctions that have been the subject of considerable discussion in the "higher sentence" debate of current linguistics (cf. Ross, 1969; Anderson, 1971; Erdmann, 1977). Indeed, it could even be argued (cf. Lightfoot, 1974) that our proposal would amount to "restoring" predications that have been submerged in the course of linguistic history.

It will be seen that Nuclear English is conceived as having great power but also as exercising drastic constraints. Not only is the language to be learned by the non-native carefully and explicitly restricted; so equally must the language of the native speaker be constrained to a precisely corresponding extent when he is using Nuclear English as an international medium. A tall order? Yes, but surely more than a mere pipe dream if we consider the continuous thought that has been given to these issues from Francis Bacon onwards—and if we take seriously the issue of international needs.

The word international was coined nearly 200 years ago by a man whose mortal remains, clothed and seated, are on prominent display in University College London. Jeremy Bentham's utilitarianism explicitly and emphatically embraced questions of linguistic engineering. He was impressed by Francis Bacon's observation that learning suffers "distemper" through the fact that words effectively mask and obscure the "weight of matter" that should be at the centre of our attention (*Advancement of Learning*, 1605). Bentham based his concern for the clarification of linguistic expression on the great tradition that extended from Bacon, through Comenius, Mersenne, Wilkins, Leibniz, Berkeley, to Horne Tooke in his own day. Indeed he strove (vainly, as it turned out) to have appointed as the first Professor of English in London the polyglot John Bowring who was keen on the notion of establishing a universal language.

The "great tradition" was seriously disrupted by the advent of comparative philology in the early nineteenth century, and the subsequent development of phonetics—in part supportive of it, in part directed in the opposite direction: the examination of substance features in living languages. This in turn gave a different emphasis in language teaching (towards speech fluency, measured especially in terms of phonetic accuracy), while the embracing by the universities of these twin branches of inquiry, phonology and comparative philology, as the dominant foci of intellectual excitement, had the effect of pushing philosophical linguistics and universalism back from the footlights. Though never entirely forgotten by academic philosophers, it was only a minority of linguists who persisted with their interests, and those have been largely on the periphery of the academic establishment. One thinks of Ogden, Korzybski, Hayakawa, and the pages of ETC, etc.

With the discovery of J. L. Austin—some years after his death—and with a greater catholicity, eclecticism, and perhaps pragmatism in linguistic theory than we have known for nearly half a century, I feel that this is the time for serious re-engagement with the issues that occupied Wilkins and his successors.

NOTES

1. I am indebted to Gregory Trifonovitch for a Japanese reference of 1859 (Fukuzawa Yukichi) predicting English to be the most useful language in the world of the future.
2. There are of course further internal linguistic complexities in Norway.
3. Cf. "The British Heresy in TESL" in Fishman *et al.*, 1968: 459–76.
4. On the basis of such facts, it is clearly a matter of internal policy for governments (in India, Nigeria, and the many other countries in this position) to decide the variety of indigenized English "to be taught in their educational systems, weighing the immediate local needs of the many against the wider needs of those who must in addition master a form of English current in international use". It need scarcely be added that this question arises only in countries making use of English for internal purposes. Other "national" varieties of English are of course equally discernible; but while "Japanese English", "German English", "Russian English" may be facts of performance linguistics, there is no reason for setting them up as facts of institutional linguistics or as models for the learners in the countries.
5. It is worth noting, however, that acrolectal English in such countries as India achieves this universality by looking outward (in contrast to the basilects) for its standards.
6. Simplification of the language, that is. Predicting failure nearly thirty years ago, George Bernard Shaw saw a way out in simplification of the teaching. In pleading for rationalization in the teaching of English as a common world language, he was ready to encourage wholesale pidginization, and thought that teachers effectively sold the pass by setting their sights too high. "All teachers should bear in mind that better is the enemy of good enough, and perfection not possible on any terms. Language . . . should not be taught beyond the point at which the speaker is understood" (*Atlantic Monthly*, **186**, October 1950, p. 62). This presupposes a highly simplistic view of comprehensibility, and in the context of an unrestricted and uncontrolled concept of "English", Shaw's prescription would probably be worse than valueless. In the context of a strictly limited lexicon, however, comprehensibility—phonetic and graphic alike—becomes less of an imponderable, and at any rate many would agree with Shaw that the teacher's goal of getting his students to achieve native-like control of a foreign language is a dangerous chimera. A somewhat analogous point has been strenuously made by Professor Takao Suzuki (*Japan Times*, Tokyo, 24 June 1979), arguing (a) that it is wasteful to teach English as widely as at present in Japan, and (b) that the English taught should be a simplified form ("Englic"), based on non-native usage.
7. Despite the ingenuity and (often) very attractive features that such inventions may display. Cf. the little known interglossa described in quite fascinating detail in a Pelican book so titled by Lancelot Hogben (Harmondsworth 1943). Hogben's sketchy handling of modality is of some interest: pp. 126f.
8. But see G. Stein, "Nuclear English: Reflections on the Structure of its Vocabulary", *Poetica*, **10** (Tokyo, 1979).
9. They must not of course be exaggerated. In the first place, there are grossly overloaded

modality systems in other languages beside English, and the same analogies and "metaphors" are very generally involved. Secondly, pragmatic factors (including common sense) often preclude misunderstanding: May I go? is unlikely to be epistemic since a person does not ask other people about what in the nature of things he must know better than anyone else. Thirdly, in many instances modal properties effectively merge, however theoretically distinct they may be: "He can leave immediately" cannot normally involve possibility without simultaneously involving permission.

10. In this connection, it would be worth examining the implications of current work by Gordon Wells of Bristol on the order and rate of acquiring modal expression in children and on the types and distribution of modal values expressed in parent-child interaction.

11. In the present programmatic outline, the specific properties of the optimal paraphrases must be ignored. Among the formidable topics for study, however, is the nature of deontic passives like "is obliged", "is permitted" and the question of specifying agency.

REFERENCES

ANDERSON, J. (1971) "Some Proposals Concerning the Modal Verbs in English", *Edinburgh Studies in English and Scots*, ed. A. J. Aitken, *et al.*, London.

ERDMANN, P. (1977) "On Deriving Deontic Modals", *Linguistics*, **192**.

FISHMAN, J. *et al.* (1968) *Language Problems in Developing Nations.* New York.

HARE, R. M. (1970) "Meaning and Speech Acts", *Philosophical Review*, **79**.

KACHRU, B. (1976) "Indian English: A Sociolinguistic Profile of a Transplanted Language", *Studies in Language Learning* I (Urbana).

LIGHTFOOT, D. W. (1974) "The Diachronic Analysis of English Modals", *Historical Linguistics* I, ed. J. M. Anderson and C. Jones, Edinburgh.

LYONS, J. (1977) *Semantics*, Cambridge.

PALMER, F. R. (1974) *The English Verb*, London.

QUIRK, R. (1972) *The English Language and Images of Matter*, London.

QUIRK, R., GREENBAUM, S., LEECH, G., SVARTVIK, J. (1972) *A Grammar of Contemporary English*, London.

QUIRK, R. (1978) "Aspects of English as an International Language", *Sproglaereren*, **9**.

ROSS, J. R. (1969) "Auxiliaries as Main Verbs", *Studies in Philosophical Linguistics* I, ed. W. Todd, Evanston.

STREVENS, P. (1977) *New Orientations in the Teaching of English*, Oxford.

"SEMI-ENGLISH" AND THE BASIC REQUIREMENTS OF SCIENTIFIC COMMUNICATION

P. H. NANCARROW

Literary and Linguistic Computing Centre, Cambridge University

One of the strongest spurs to human endeavour is idleness. The human animal is notoriously lazy, and if he can do something more easily, that's the way he's going to do it. And that's what happened to me when I was asked to translate some Chinese geological texts some years ago. I agreed willingly, but as soon as I sat down with the text and the dictionaries I was faced with a problem. Although a scientist, I am not a geologist, and I didn't know the terminology. Now Chinese, as well as being a language which is daunting because it uses characters—and lots of them—is also difficult because in the written form there is no variation in the width of the gaps between the characters, whether you are inside a multi-character word or between adjacent words. Unlike the situation in a Western book, where we have nice clear white spaces between words, so that we can tell which the words are even if we don't know them, in a Chinese text the situation is quite simply that if you don't know what the words are in a given string of characters, then you don't even know which are the words, because the typography itself doesn't show you. So, even the mere task of looking things up in a dictionary can be incredibly difficult, and as I was involved with the development of equipment for entering Chinese character texts into computer systems, it occurred to me that this equipment could be used to compile a bilingual dictionary of technical Chinese, so that any text could be put into a computer and scanned against the dictionary to see which combinations of characters could possibly constitute words. Early experiments, done by hand, were very promising; not only was I able to print out the English glosses for the technical Chinese words, but I also found that it was possible to exploit the form of the written Chinese language and process the functional and everyday words as well, so that the output was in the format of a continuous coherent text using English words. When the output was handed to the geologist, it provided him with a very good account of the content of the original text—and in fact more recent experimentation has brought the process to a stage where it is converting in excess of 95% of the content of the original for assimilation by the reader.

Now, it is the output of this process which is referred to as "semi-English". This is a term coined at Cambridge specifically to define this particular form of output, and as far as I know it has not been used elsewhere. It simply indicates in a general way that the output is related to English, in that it uses English words, but is not what would normally be regarded as standard English.

On another point of terminology, I want to stress the difference between the ideas of "translation" and "conversion". Many people assume that my work is machine translation, but I would not agree with this assessment, since my understanding is that machine translation is a system where one attempts by program to analyse an input text on the basis of its syntax so as to form a machine representation of the input text within the computer, and to synthesize the output text from the internal representation according to further syntactic criteria. The syntactic aspect is the main problem of machine translation, and results in the rather low efficiency, around 75–80%, since the flexibility of human language leads to difficulties in the implementation of automatic syntactic analysis. By contrast, my process virtually abandoned the syntactic approach, relying very heavily on the content of the original text (and thus in a sense being semantically based), and I use the word "conversion" to describe it, as I do not believe that it is accurate to describe such a process, with its origins in a simple dictionary matching system, as "translation". I therefore use the word "conversion" rigorously in the present content when referring to the semi-English process.

It is implausible at first glance to consider that a matching process, with whatever modifications, would give a degree of success of the level which has in fact been observed with semi-English, and discussion beyond the scope of this paper explains what I believe to be the reasons for the success in the particular field of technical Chinese. My initial reaction was that written technical Chinese was a very special case, not least because of its use of Characters. The important thing about Chinese text in this respect is that each character has associated with it a given unit of meaning. Even the functional and relational parts of a sentence have to be expressed in characters, and so the whole text can be processed as information rather than language, on the basis of the content of each character—or group of characters in the case of multi-character words. It is this feature of concentration on the content of a text which gives semi-English its relevance to the study of English for Special Purposes. Much research in ESP has involved the study of existing English texts, which scholars have analysed to find out what range of vocabulary and syntax is used by scientists when writing in English. Obviously this analysis is useful, but one disadvantage is that the texts have been written by people whose native tongue is English. They therefore have great resources of vocabulary and syntax at their disposal and one is looking at what they actually write, as opposed to what they might have written if they had been trying to do it with a minimum of language resources, so that the results of the analysis are to a certain degree subjective. My approach is that in the production of semi-English, language has been reduced by a number of processes which are not directly related to standard English. The texts in Chinese are processed on the basis of their logical content, and therefore semi-English itself represents a medium which is based on content rather than on language. Moving on from this, as I explained in the paper, it appears that the format of semi-English closely reflects the thought processes common to scientists when dealing with their scientific specializations. For these reasons I think it is valuable to study semi-English and its implications for the rational construction of English language sub-sets for special purposes.

From this you will appreciate that the process of production of semi-English is working in regions very close to the fundamental nature of scientific expression. Firstly, the process operates on information rather than language, and in dealing with content in this way we are concentrating on the substance rather than the form. Secondly, the constraint of working within the region of shared knowledge in a given field immediately concentrates semi-English into that part of language specifically concerned with scientific and technical communication. Furthermore, and getting to a deeper level of investigation, the process appears to be identifying that part of the internal map of the world which relates to specialist topics, and it is here that I think the significance of semi-English is manifest.

So far, I have been talking about semi-English itself, from inside the hermetic container within which it has been developing. The problem at this stage is to find ways of looking at semi-English from outside to discover whether or not it is a valid approach. There are now two kinds of evidence which have a bearing on this question.

The first kind of evidence is the result of the experiment, which is being carried out at the Cavendish Laboratory at Cambridge. The full results of that experiment are not yet available, the physicists who have volunteered to do the task are still working, but the preliminary results have begun to emerge, and they are consistent with the assumption that there is a matching between a physicist's training and the way in which he handles semi-English. The sentence structures build up in a very regular and consistent way, and although it is too early to do a statistical analysis of the results, it is very significant that the results from drafting in the field of physics are broadly comparable to the results referred to in the paper in drafts produced by Dr. C. P. Hughes of the University Geology Department and Mr. King, Assistant Taxonomist at the University Botanic Gardens. They produced their semi-English drafts as paraphrases of existing standard English, but in the Cavendish I have tried to get nearer to the mind of the physicist by providing tasks which he has to assemble in his imagination. The format of the semi-English from this type of task is analogous to that from the other workers, but there is a slightly greater "mathematical" precision in handling the text in the case of the Cavendish output. My impression is that when the full results from the Cavendish experiment are analysed, they will demonstrate a correlation between the semi-English styles of physicists working independently on similar tasks.

The second kind of evidence is provided by the results of a recent extension of the scope of the language conversion technique beyond the initial work from Chinese into semi-English, into an area well outside the hermetic container. The problem in discussing this extension is that it looks even more like machine translation than the original process, and I must ask you to bear in mind the earlier discussion of the difference between the terms "translation" and "conversion".

Once success in the semi-English process was evident, there was a tendency on the part of observers to assume that the conversion could simply be put into reverse to convert English into Chinese. This assumption overlooked the differences between English and Chinese, and my view at the time that Chinese was a special case made me reluctant to embark on experiments in that direction. There was simply no evidence to suggest that simple reversal was any more practicable than attempting to unbake a cake. However, he who pays the piper calls the tune, and earlier this year I proposed a compromise plan, to paraphrase an English text into semi-English and use the computer to convert the semi-English into semi-Chinese. That was as far as I was prepared to go. However, when I sat down to do the job, the missing evidence began to appear. It became apparent that the paraphrasing I was doing by hand, and particularly the annotations which I was inserting in the original text, could in fact in the majority of cases be done automatically by the computer, not using syntactic criteria, nor even many semantic clues, but working at a level which, on the analogy of deep and surface structure, I would call superficial structure, picking up textual rather than linguistic clues. Encouraged by this appreciation, I in fact went beyond my original compromise and moved directly to the conversion of the input English text into semi-Chinese by a fully automatic computer process. To my surprise, and against all the odds, it worked. I was flabbergasted when it happened, and couldn't really believe my eyes. Working from my home, with the computer terminal coupled *via* the telephone line, the response was very slow, and it was agonizing to watch the Chinese output being built up on the screen, because gradually the structures came out correctly, clause by clause. It was intensely nerve-wracking, but it was working.

Now, for that to happen, in a process based on the analysis derived for the original semi-English conversion, indicates that the analysis is closely related to the fundamental structure of written technical materials. If, as appears to be the case, the semi-English approach is able more generally to segment a text on the basis of its content, sufficiently accurately for that content to be represented in another language, then it is getting very near indeed to the nuts and bolts of technical communication.

When pondering these results it seemed clear that in some sense the conversion process preserves not only the sense of the individual sentence components of the original text, but also the information about their inter-relationships. If this were true, then it could be reasonably speculated that the output language could be something other than Chinese. This again, for reasons of time, remained as no more than speculation, but the piper once again exercised his prerogative, specifying this time that the output should be in an inflecting language, perhaps Russian. Again I compromised, on the ground that one should learn to walk before attempting to run, and I am currently experimenting with the conversion of English into semi-Norwegian. The reason for this choice is twofold. Firstly, and more importantly, Norwegian is an inflecting language, although its inflections are less complex than in Russian. Secondly, it is one of the languages which I have studied. The current experiment thus provides an opportunity to study the problems of handling inflection in the conversion process, in anticipation of future extension of the technique to more complex cases. So far the experiment shows that it is possible to convert from English to semi-Norwegian, not only in respect of the basic roots of words, but—and this is another surprising feature—to produce appropriate inflectional forms in the Norwegian without a step of true syntactic analysis. Now again, this is all very much against the odds. A year ago I would have said that what I have just told you would be impossible. Nevertheless, the case of semi-Norwegian, taken together with the case of semi-Chinese, implies that the semi-English approach is giving a fundamental view of the basic logical structures which seem to underlie scientific and technical discourse.

If the experiments at the Cavendish Laboratory, and the extensions of the conversion technique beyond the original case, continue to justify the assumptions about the fundamental nature of the semi-English process, then semi-English itself will be indicated as a particularly apposite source of information in the field of design of reduced English for special purposes. This is not to say that semi-English is at present in an advanced state. Confirmation of its basic validity was sought at the earliest stage at which this could be done, and continuing work, particularly on the structural side, is necessary. Nor would I say that semi-English itself would form a teachable medium of communication. Nevertheless, I believe that the lessons which can be drawn from the semi-English approach are very relevant indeed to the question of ESP.

ACKNOWLEDGEMENT

I am indebted to the English-Speaking Union for their continuing sponsorship of this work, and to the Shell Grants Committee for the financial support which has carried the project to its present point. Within Cambridge University I would acknowledge the assistance I have received from the Computing services, especially in advice on computer graphics, and the various draftsmen in the scientific disciplines I have mentioned. Not least, I would also highlight the patient support and assistance afforded by my wife, particularly in providing a critical eye and ear in the process of editing and presenting this and other reports; without this help, you might have found yourselves listening to a treatise in demi-semi-English!

2. *Specific Cases*

COMMUNICATIONS AT SEA

F. F. WEEKS

Plymouth Polytechnic

From the earliest days of recorded history, man has always striven to improve
communications. With respect to ships. this has progressed by slow and pain-
ful stages, beginning with methods which depended completely on sound—
first the human voice and then other, louder noise producing instruments
such as bugles and drums. But sound signals, especially under sea conditions,
are notoriously unreliable, and only have a low predictable range. Even an
adverse wind can render a sound signal inaudible! Visual signals were then
developed using flags, semaphore flags and, latterly, flashing lights. These
methods were all that were available at the end of the last century, and had
three things in common:

  (i) They were slow.
 (ii) They were short range.
(iii) They were mainly used between ships, or fleets of ships, of the same
      nationality.

   Discussing these points in more detail:

(i)   (a) Using flags

           There are two possibilities. In the first, a series of flags is produc-
           ed, each with a single letter meaning, one for "A", one for "B"
           and so on. A plain language message can then be made up, the
           flags hoisted, and the message passed. This method has two dis-
           advantages. First, if the flags are to be seen clearly they have to
           be large. Thus the practical number on one joist (on one signal
           halliard) is limited to about five. This means that even a short
           sentence occupies every signal halliard in the ship. Reading such
           a message is easy, but sending it is extremely tedious and slow,
           remembering that a Merchant Ship has very little manpower in-
           deed. To make a signal "I require assistance" in plain language,
           on a Merchant ship, would probably require well over five mi-
           nutes of frantic work.

Secondly a code can be produced, in which a single flag, or small groups of flags is substituted for a group of words. Thus in the International Code of Signals the single flag "V" is substituted for the group of words "I require assistance". In this case, the hoisting a single flag would require about one minute, taking into account the "do it yourself" nature of Merchant ship bridge manning.

(b) Using Semaphore Flags

This method has now fallen out of use on Merchant ships due to its extreme short range capability discussed in (ii). It consists of a code transmitted by hand-held flags, each arm position indicating a letter of the alphabet. In Merchant ship use, a maximum transmission speed of some ten words (50 letters) per minute could be achieved.

(c) Using Flashing Lights (The Morse code)

This method is still in use today, but is falling more and more into disuse. It has the advantage that, unlike flag signalling, it can be used day and night. But it has two disadvantages. First, it is comparatively slow, eight words per minute being the officially accepted norm for Merchant ships, and, second, it requires the undivided attention of the operator. On a Merchant ship, this is inevitably the Officer of the Watch, who therefore cannot continue to keep a proper look-out whilst using flashing light apparatus.

(ii)   (a) *Using Flags*

Requires: Daylight
Good visibility
Range less than 5 miles.

(b) *Using Semaphore Flags*

Requires: Daylight
Good visibility
Range less than one mile.

(c) *Using Flashing Light*

Requires: Good visibility
Visual range between ships.

(iii) *Nationality*

    (a) *Using Flags*

The receiving station must know the letter of the alphabet which each flag used by the transmitting ship is equivalent to. For example: Red Burgee = "B". Using this knowledge, a receiving ship can easily understand a plain language message *provided* that the sender and the receiver share the same mother tongue. If not, then the problem of translation immediately arises. Thus, for a non-English speaking person, the understanding of a flag signal involves two stages:

(1) Placing an alphabetical meaning to each flag.
(2) Translating the received message into speaker's own language.

A failure at either stage would result in a failure in communications. This need not, of course, involve a non-native English speaker. The flags used by the Royal Navy are different in alphabetical meaning, colour and shape to those used by British Merchant ships. Therefore, if a Royal Navy ship wishes to communicate with a British Merchant ship, she must use the flags of the International Code. Her own, Naval, flags are unintelligable to the Merchant man. For a non-native English speaker, translation would be a relatively easy process, depending only on an ability to translate the written word at a very leisurely pace.

Because of the dual problems of lack of speed in transmitting a signal by plain language and translating the message on receipt, the International Code of Signals was introduced. This well-known code works as follows:

1. A series of messages is graded according to importance.
2. Flag signals are allocated to the messages. One flag signal for the most important, two flag signals for less important, and so on.

The Practical steps are as follows:

    (a) The transmitting ship encodes her message into the appropriate flag signal.
    (b) The receiving ship reads the signal and decodes into her own language.

This method works well, but the method is labour-intensive and, for modern use, very slow indeed. Even using every navigating officer on the ship, it is doubtful if a Merchant ship could achieve a signal rate of one word per minute, if more than a single hoist were used. Since, under modern conditions, the officer of the watch is completely alone on the bridge, the method is quite impractical for everyday use.

The traditional methods described above were the only ones available to the ship until the advent of radio. It should be noted that all these methods were (and are) operated by bridge personnel. That is, by the navigating officer of the watch.

With the advent of radio, the ships' principal method of communication passed out of the direct control of the officer of the watch, and into the control of a specialist, the Radio Officer. It is interesting to consider the necessary stages in sending a message by Radio Telegraphy (morse) between two stations of the same nationality:

1. Transmitting ship writes out message in plain language.
2. Transmitting ship encodes message into Morse, transmits.
3. Receiving ship receives Morse, decodes into plain language written message.

If the transmitting ship is sending a signal to a foreign station, or wishes to maintain some sort of secrecy, he will encode the signal, either into the International Code of Radio Signals, or some other, private, code. The stages are then:

1. Transmitting ship writes out message in plain language.
2. Transmitting ship encodes message into Code.
3. Transmitting ship encodes message into Morse, transmits.
4. Receiving ship receives Morse, decodes into Code.
5. Receiving ship decodes Code into plain language (own Mother tongue).

In both cases, the task is one of writing and comprehension, and does not involve the spoken word at all. Thus it is not surprising that Radio Operators are highly technically skilled personnel, who have no special language training whatever.

Thus, until the decade 1960–1970 the communication system on most Merchant ships was as follows:

Flag Signalling (International Code) ⎫	
Semaphore Flags ⎬	Officer of the watch.
Morse Flashing ⎭	
Radio Telegraphy	Radio Officer

The great advances made in VHF radio during World War II, in the aircraft industry, had not been applied to Merchant ships, and the long range Radio Telephone had not arrived. So, if we consider the year 1965, communications on a Merchant ship were almost exactly the same as before the First World War, apart for some detailed advances in equipment. Very few ships were equipped with any new communications systems whatever.

Before considering communications developments since 1965 let us look at the educational and national background of some typical Merchant ship bridge officers, particularly with regard to language. At the end of the Second World War it is fair to say that the sea was an English speaking environment. Nearly all Merchant officers spoke English, either as their native tongue or as their adopted tongue. Further, very few native English speaking officers spoke any foreign language at all. Not only had their education been science based, but they knew, by instinct, that everyone in the world speaks English, anyway. This attitude persists today, in Britain, since there is no requirement whatever for a British bridge officer to learn any foreign language. In North West Europe, after the Second World War, some enlightened educational decisions were taken. One of these was that every school child should learn a foreign language, to a really acceptable level. In most cases, this language was English. Most North West European Captains and Officers under 45 years in age therefore have a command of English which is impressive, and which is a direct result of their national education systems.

But, paradoxically, the rise in prosperity of Europe and Scandinavia has produced a fall in the total numbers of ships flying the flags of their real European owner country. This is because the wage of crews are just too high, and, if the shipping company concerned is to remain profitable, some reduction in crew costs must be made. This is a trend which has been in evidence for some years, the latest manifestation of which has been the "flagging out" of the Cunard Countess and the Cunard Princess. Because of their very high skill and "value for money" factor, European officers are frequently kept on board, with foreign or multi-national crews. But this is not always the case.

Consider, for example, an underdeveloped country which is rich in minerals, which have always been carried in the ships of other countries. Then, as a matter of Government policy, it is decided that the country should have a Merchant fleet, manned by nationals of that country. Perhaps it may be possible in, let us say, two years, to train existing Naval personnel to form the officer nucleus of that fleet. But spoken English cannot usually be learned in two years, and really depends on there having been a suitable education system in the country concerned. In many cases this simply does not exist, for a multiplicity of reasons, but usually because the demands on a limited national budget are just too many. In such circumstances languages often suffer, whilst the sciences are favoured.

It may also happen that the education system in this underdeveloped country may favour the written word over the spoken word, as happens in several far Eastern countries.

So if we examine the manpower situation of bridge officers today, we find a different composition entirely to that at the end of the Second World War. Gone is the predominance of the native English speaker, even though English remains the official International language of the sea. Instead, we find a very large and increasing proportion of non-native English speakers, some of whom are fluent in the spoken and written word in English, some in the written word only, and some not at all.

If the communications system had remained static, as it was up to 1960 (that is, Flags, Morse and Radio) then this would have produced little problem, because, as we have seen, all communications were through the written word and not the spoken

But, during the decade 1960–1970 an enormous technical advance took place in communications at sea. The VHF radio transmitter, long in use on aircraft, started to appear in significant numbers on ships.

This produced many immediate advantages, some of which were:

   (i) A reliable voice communication to the visible horizon, in all weathers, by day and night.

  (ii) The return of communications, for many applications, from the Radio Officer to the Bridge Officer.

 (iii) An increase in speed of transmission of messages over all methods, previously within the charge of the bridge officer.

 (iv) A rapid and effective means of transmitting emergency, safety and anti-collision messages within the charge of the officer of the watch.

Technically, all these advantages were, and are, valid, but several important factors had not been considered. For example:

  (a) Even today, only a tiny minority of Merchant bridge officers have any formal training in the use of a VHF. In Britain, for example, this is not compulsory.

  (b) Because of lack of training, many users of VHF have "the telephone syndrome" imagining that they have a "direct line" to the receiving ship. This often produces undisciplined conversations.

  (c) The range and popularity of VHF has produced crowding on many of the allocated frequencies, often with the result that emergency calls are very difficult to make.

  (d) For a bridge officer, previously used to the highly directional Morse searchlight, the non-directional VHF is a little strange in use. Thus unless positive identification can be made, a signal can be made to one ship, and a second ship responds.

But in the English Speaking Union we are mainly concerned with language and how it can best be used. It is in this sphere that the effects of VHF have mainly been felt.

Imagine a bridge officer from an underdeveloped country, as previously described. Before, his ship was not fitted with VHF and the only communications demands made on him were via the written word, and at a maximum speed of ten words per minute (semaphore). Always, a pause for coding and de-coding could be obtained.

Then a VHF set is fitted, and, with no training, our bridge officer commences to use it. After much preparation, he makes his first ship-to-ship call, calling a British ship. The reply will be at something over *80* words per minute, in colloquial English which our foreign officer has never heard, and therefore does not understand.

In ordinary circumstances this may be treated as a humourous incident, particularly by a Briton, since it gives him confirmation of his language superiority. But to a non-native English speaker it can never be humourous. And in an emergency situation such language difficulties can be a potential disaster.

In fact, demands are made by VHF upon the language abilities of bridge officers which only those educated to the highest standards by the most sophisticated educational systems are able to meet. For those without the benefits of such an education, 80 words a minute of colloquial English is a completely impossible goal. What, then, can be done?

As in most aspects of life, a disaster had to occur before action was taken. Unfortunately, such an incident was not long in occurring.

In 1967 the Danish ship *Elsa Priess* sank in the North Sea, with the loss of all hands. This was the first major accident which could be directly attributed to a failure in VHF communications, and aroused the international shipping community to an awareness of some of the language difficulties, which this "new" communication system produced. Eventually, in 1977, the publication *The Standard Marine Navigational Vocabulary* was produced by the Intergovernmental Maritime Consultative Organization (IMCO), an organization of the United Nations. This was a valuable first step towards solving the communication problem which, in the ten years since the *Elsa Priess*, had multiplied many times over.

Before messages can be categorized and classified there are some really major differences between the use of VHF at sea and in the air which should be considered. These are:

1. Air traffic is *controlled* by air traffic controllers, on the ground, and aircraft pilots *must* obey. Ships' Captains may be *advised* by a shore station as to what they *should* do. Only in one place in the world, in peacetime, are they *controlled*, or *told* what to do. This is at Ushant, off West Britanny, as a result of the Amoco Cadiz disaster. This means that a completely different style of English is necessary in each case.
2. *All* aircraft pilots must be trained and qualified in the use of VHF, and in the use of the special "Procedures and Phraseology" based on English. Without this qualification they do not fly. This applies to all

nationalities. On ships, only the Radio Operator is trained and qualified to use the VHF. But he is not the normal user. The bridge officer is, and he is untrained and unqualified, unless voluntarily. Thus, in some countries, notably Britain, there is no requirement to even have a working knowledge of the Standard Marine Vocabulary. Paradoxically, in many foreign countries such a knowledge is compulsory.

Messages sent by VHF may be categorized under the following headings, in decreasing order of importance:

(a) Emergency (Distress) messages.
(b) Security messages.
(c) Messages necessary for the safe navigation of the ship.
(d) Messages necessary for the business affairs of the ship.
(e) Redundant and trivial messages.

These categories, and some examples, are further examined below:

(a) *Emergency (Distress) Messages*
The safety of all the persons on board a ship is of prime importance, and all emergency services should be, and most are, directed to this end. The large amount and variety of dangerous cargoes carried at sea make it essential that the crew should be rescued as quickly as possible, by the most modern methods.

Thus we require:

(i) A guaranteed "free passage" for the distress message, that is, a separate frequency allocated exclusively for distress messages, to make sure that they can be heard without interference. Unfortunately such a frequency does not exist, the same frequency being used for calling and distress. This can frequently mean that a distress call is obliterated by several other ships calling shore stations at the same time.
(ii) Absolute clarity of message, both in format and in presentation, but also, of course, in factual information.

Such a call (actual example) would read:

MAYDAY, MAYDAY, MAYDAY. This is foreign ship NONSUCH. MAYDAY, MAYDAY. Nonsuch, Nonsuch. In collision with other ship. Making water in the engine room. Approximate position is about seven miles Easterly of Southwold. Over please.

Most of this message is quite straightforward, and could be transmitted using the Standard Marine Vocabulary. Then it would appear as:

MAYDAY, MAYDAY, MAYDAY. This is foreign ship Nonsuch. I need help. I have been in collision. My position is seven miles East of Southwold. Over.

The phrase "making water in the engine room" does not appear in the Vocabulary, and neither does the word "approximate". This highlights one of the disadvantages of the Vocabulary. It is rather like a phrase book in that it often does not contain exactly what one wants to say, but only something rather similar.

Nevertheless, although the Vocabulary has its limitations in this category, it is a valuable step forward. Or would be if it were used by all nations.

(b) *Security Messages*

These may be defined as messages affecting the safety of navigation for all the ships in the area, and not just that of the transmitting ship. Similarly, these messages contain information which may lead to the contamination of the environment. In other words, to pollution.

For most members of the population pollution, and its effects, are far more important than the safety of the crew members on board. Therefore, the general public may consider that messages in this category are more important even than distress messages. For example, there was never really any question of the crew of the *Amoco Cadiz* being in ultimate danger. But the communications passing between the ship and New York, which ultimately made it inevitable that the ship would ground, really decided whether the Britanny beaches would be polluted or not.

(c) *Safe Navigation*

"Safety of navigation" includes the conduct of vessels which are in danger of colliding with one another. VHF, if properly used, can be of great assistance in such circumstances. But the following sequence *must* be adhered to, otherwise there could be a communication failure, and, subsequently, a collision.

(i) Clear and positive identification of each ship by the other.
(ii) Clear and concise message.
(iii) Positive action in strict accordance with the content of the message.

The following incident occurred in Swedish waters. Vessel A (20,000 Tons) had a pilot on board and was on a North-Westerly course. She collided with B (5000 Tons) coming from a crossing channel from starboard. Both channels were in the archipelago and were comparatively narrow. Visibility was limited by the mainland and the islands between the channels. The vessels sighted each other about 4.5 minutes before the collision at a distance of 0.6M. Both were then about 0.6M from the point of collision and made relatively high speed considering the visibility. Just after A had sighted B, A's pilot called B and spoke to B's Master. According to A's version, the conversation was as follows:

A. If you can see me, Take it easy because I can't stop.
B. Yes, I can see you. You are welcome.

According to B, the conversation was like this:

A. Now you have to watch out because here we come.
B. Yes, I see you. All right.

Both ships were found to be to blame for the collision, which is hardly surprising, considering the ambiguous nature of their conversation.

The British Government issue strict instructions that *positive* identification *must* be made before a course alteration is made. This is, of course, because the VHF is non-directional, and therefore the wrong ship may alter course!

In simple cases, the Standard Marine Navigational Vocabulary is useful but not entirely adequate in the construction of "anti-collision" messages. A logical improvement would be to carefully research the exact requirements of the VHF in the collision situation, among others. Navigational equipment may also be included in this section:

British Ship: Have you got any charts of the area. Do you know there are many oil rigs in the vicinity of the anchorage. Have you got charts of that area? Over.
French Ship: No. We have no chart just for this area.

Surely this is an important navigational message? But the Vocabulary cannot deal with it.

(d) *Business messages*
These include messages necessary for the everyday efficient and profitable operation of the ship, mostly being used when a ship is in port approaches. Although not as essential as the preceding three classes of messages, they contain far more variety of language. No "Code" or "Vocabulary" exists, and it is in this area that the severest tests of language ability take place. For the underdeveloped countries this may present a very real commercial handicap, both from the point of view of the bridge officer and the harbour official.

Again, careful research into language needs is the only solution.

To summarise:
Almost every ship now has a VHF. One commercial company supplies over 2000 sets per year for yachts. The VHF frequencies are becoming more and more crowded. No special VHF language exists, but a "Vocabulary" does exist, in the form of a phrase book.

What can be done?
Procedural discipline with VHF is a matter for the Maritime authorities in the various countries concerned. But language should concern all of us, because it is an International communication tool, which affects everyone but, most vitally, those who serve in ships.

The first essential is a special language which is specifically designed for use at sea, under all circumstances, is concise, and easy to learn. It would, in fact be a Basic English of the sea, having a carefully researched vocabulary and a simple sentence structure.

Such a language would be of enormous help to the underdeveloped countries, whose bridge officers have, perhaps, little desire to undertake the enormous task which "the whole of English" represents. Instead, they wish to learn only that English which is necessary for their safety, the safety of others, and the efficient conduct of their shipping operation.

The language—let us call it "Seaspeak"—would be a truly worthwhile project which would improve safety and efficiency in international communications. At this moment, it stands before the United Nations as an official IMCO project request. Such a project would truly enable bridge officers of all nations to communicate with each other effectively, as the pilots of aircraft have been able to do for many years.

DEFINING AND ASSESSING LEVELS OF JOB-RELATED PERFORMANCE, THE CASE OF SKF

C. ST. J. YATES

English Language Teaching Development Unit Ltd (ELTDU)

> "We make money by making motor cars; we don't make money by teaching employees English."

This remark, made within the last six months by the training director of Ford in Germany is indicative of the attitude of many training managers responsible for language training programmes within their companies in Europe. While attitudes to language training clearly vary from company to company, there are certain underlying beliefs that most, we find, hold in common. These beliefs can broadly be summarized as follows.

While the typical multi-national, or indeed export-oriented company accepts the need for language training, it expects that training to be related to the needs of the company itself; in other words, to the needs of a particular job or group of jobs.

Company training managers tend to see English language training as one area among many in which employees may or may not need training to make their performance on the job more effective. They are therefore talking about "language training" with an objective in view, as distinct from "language teaching" for purely social, cultural or educational purposes.

The second point characteristically made by training managers is that they themselves wish to lay down the language training objectives for their employees. They are sceptical of having a language training programme defined for them by linguists or teachers unless that programme is shown to be demonstrably relevant. While it is certainly true that many training managers cannot lay down objectives or define their needs in terms that will be understood by the language teacher, the feeling persists that they know what they want, even if this is only expressed in terms of "Don't teach them grammar, teach them to speak".

Perhaps most importantly is the attitude that English language training must be cost-effective. When a company places an employee on an in-company training scheme or, perhaps, sends that employee to a British language school, it is costing that company money. For that money, the company wishes to have a result. It is, in effect, buying a service or product in exactly the same way that it buys steel for manufacturing purposes. It should, perhaps, be pointed out that the money spent by the company consists not solely of the direct costs of the training given, but also the indirect costs of removing that employee from his job.

A final attitude that one frequently finds when dealing with company training programmes is that to the English language itself. Typically, English is seen as a means to an end, not an end in itself. Further it is seen as a means of international communication between non-native speakers of the language. It is not seen as bound to British or American business practice, cultural heritage or political institutions.

The desire to have a language training programme that is directly related to the job requirements of employees, that is cost-effective, and whose results can be readily assessed does, of course, presuppose a means for establishing such a scheme. It was this lack of a readily available means that led SKF (Aktiebolaget Svenska Kullagerfabrik) to approach ELTDU for a solution.

In SKF, as in many companies, it is often necessary for management to know the level of English required by employees, and on occasion to know the level of English required if they are to carry out particular activities effectively. Situations that require such knowledge are, for example, when a subsidiary company is asked to delegate one or two employees for a meeting outside their own country; when the company wishes to send one or more engineers to make a technical presentation to a potential customer.

This need to know an employee's language ability is not of course restricted to one-off events such as these two examples. When recruiting new employees to posts that, by their very nature, involve a certain mastery over English, it is important for the company to have a means of assessing potential recruits' existing ability. Similarly, when considering transferring an employee from one company to another within a group, it is important to know whether that person can perform in English in his new post before he takes it up.

Within SKF there were other problems, such as the need for a common means of assessing performance throughout the group. Conventional EFL labels such as Intermediate, Advanced etc. tended to relate solely to local language teachers' ideas as to what constituted Intermediate and Advanced, and these varied considerably from country to country where SKF were active. These could not be used as an objective criterion for measuring language ability as related to job functions.

A further problem within the SKF group related to the question of cost-effectiveness. The company was spending a very great deal of money on English language training, both on in-company schemes and on sending employees to language schools in this country. The results were extremely disappointing, leaving the company with the feeling that they were not getting value for the money they were spending. This was not necessarily the fault of the language schools, as SKF itself was not able to express its requirements in terms that the language school, with its limited experience of business, could readily translate into a relevant teaching programme. There was in fact a communication gap to be bridged between company and supplier, caused in the first instance by the company's inability to define its training objectives clearly, even to itself.

Also related to the question of cost-effectiveness was the problem of how much training to give an employee or group of employees. To overtrain an employee in English was, in the company's opinion, just as much a waste of money as to undertrain him. The company would no more want to overtrain than it would want to overorder raw materials for its manufacturing processes, while to undertrain meant lack of job effectiveness.

In order to assist SKF overcome these problems we at ELTDU developed a "Stages of Attainment" Scale. The Scale itself is in two parts. Firstly, there is an administrative section designed for the training department and managers within the company. This section consists of a breakdown of all the activities carried out by employees within the group that required the use of a foreign language for their performance. These activities are shown below.

INDEX TO SECTION 1

(a) *Listening and Speaking Skills*

Face-to-Face Dealings with Customers/Suppliers/Agents, etc.
Dealing with Visitors
Attending Conferences/Seminars
Verbally Relaying Information
Training
Internal Business Meetings*
External Business Meetings* and Negotiations
Making Public Statements
Use of the Telephone
Ancillary and Office Services (Typing/Translating/Interpreting)
Entertaining and Other Social Purposes

* Meeting here means a group of people convened for a business purpose.

(b) *Reading Skills*

>   Routine/Non-Routine Correspondence
>   Instructions/Requests
>   Abbreviations (Notes/Telexes/Telegrams/etc.)
>   Journals
>   PR/Press
>   Reports (including Forms and Minutes)
>   Internal Company Communications
>   Specialist Written Material (e.g. Contracts/Patents/etc.)

(c) *Writing Skills*

>   Routine/Non-Routine Correspondence
>   Instructions/Requests
>   Abbreviations (Notes/Telexes/Telegrams/etc.)
>   Journals
>   PR/Press
>   Reports (including Forms and Minutes)
>   Internal Company Communications
>   Specialist Written Material (e.g. Contracts/Patents/etc.)

Each of these activities was then broken down on an eight-point scale, where A is absolute beginner, and H is approximately native speaker. As can be seen from the following pages, each band on the Scale contains a definition of job competence to carry out that particular activity. You will also see that the activities have been grouped according to whether they require Listening/ Speaking, Reading or Writing skills.

The uses to which this part of the Scale can be put by a company are numerous. Firstly, it can be used as a means of setting training objectives, either in very precise or very broad terms. If, for example, a company wishes to train a group of ten salesmen, all of whose jobs are more or less similar, the administrator setting the training objective would first consult the index shown on the previous page. He would select those activities that he knew were important parts of his salesmen's jobs. Assuming that he chooses "Face-to-Face Dealings with Customers" as an important activity, he then turns to the breakdown of that activity shown on the following page. Of the various definitions given there he selects the one that most corresponds to the job performance required by those particular salesmen.

At this point the administrator can either say "Stage E" is my training objective for these salesmen—a broad objective has been set—or he can repeat the process with all the activities carried out in those jobs, thereby generating a detailed profile of requirements that will differentiate target stages of performance not only between the different language skills, but between different activities within those skills.

The Stages of Attainment Scale is therefore a means of setting training objectives, and by implication also a means of avoiding both undertraining and overtraining.

It can also be used as a budget tool, in that experience shows that it takes an employee on average 100 lessons to progress from one Stage to another on the Scale. Before training commences, therefore, an approximate cost can be worked out.

The second section of the Scale is designed primarily for the language teacher and language school. It consists of a set of language specifications for each Stage on the Scale. Assuming for the moment that our administrator has selected Stage E as the desired target level, and has informed the language teacher that this is the objective required, the teacher consults the language specifications for this stage. These are the language items that he will have to teach if that training objective is to be reached, in addition to those set out for the four previous Stages.

The teacher's section therefore acts as an outline syllabus. It also, however, acts as a checklist against which to assess the actual teaching materials he is considering using. If the materials do not include the language items specified, he knows that they will not enable him to reach his teaching objective without further work.

The language specifications for Stage E are given on the pages following the breakdown of the activity "Face-to-Face dealing with Customers".

Listening and Speaking

Levels	FACE-TO-FACE DEALINGS WITH CUSTOMERS/SUPPLIERS/AGENTS ETC.
A	
B	
C	CAN perform routine tasks e.g. eliciting/stating quantity of order; eliciting/quoting prices; eliciting/giving information on delivery dates; etc. Can be helpful only to the extent of referring the matter to someone else—e.g. "I'm afraid I don't know about that. I'll ask Mr. X to phone you/call". BUT cannot deal with unexpected enquiries or complex information.
D	CAN perform more specialist tasks of a fact-finding nature—e.g. establishing the nature/cause of a faulty product. Can begin to exchange opinions on things like market trends/recent developments in research PROVIDED he is dealing with a non-native speaker or an established contact. BUT his lack of polite speech formulae might create a bad impression with a native speaking stranger.
E	CAN establish business contacts. Can give detailed information in his own field—e.g. new product/research results—and can answer queries or clarify his meaning. Can sort out problems, deal with complaints, put forward proposals, sound out opinions, etc. Can deal with native speakers. BUT cannot be persuasive or get involved in an argument.
F	CAN put his point across more persuasively and can argue effectively. Can give information and answer queries on all spheres of the business. BUT may have difficulty in dealing with very awkward situations or highly sensitive issues.
G	HAS a sufficient range of language to handle delicate or complex situations.
H	CAN manipulate other people—i.e. bring them round to his way of thinking, talk them into doing what he wants. Has the language necessary to be highly articulate and persuasive.

STAGE E: Listening and Speaking

Employee should be able to:

Receive visitors and look after their needs. Deal tactfully with awkward situations.

Establish business contacts. Give detailed information in own field, answer queries, clarify meaning.

Deal with complaints, sort out problems, put forward proposals, sound out opinion, etc. (With native speakers).

Follow talks or lecture with very little difficulty and ask questions. Make an effective contribution to follow-up discussions and usefully exchange views with other participants.

Take part in all types of training programmes. Query points and ask for clarification. Verbalise his own problems and seek advice.

Instruct others how to do things (at a non-abstract level).

Pass on complex messages. Give a straightforward report of events/situations and clarify this report for his listeners.

Take part in meetings with native speakers or where non-native speakers are in the minority. Talk at length about his own sphere of responsibility. Get his point across, offer advice, raise objections, etc. (May have difficulty with some accents. May seem abrupt to a native speaker).

Use the telephone as a wider means of communication—make arrangements, clarify, report, etc. Convey and receive relatively complex messages.

Deliver a short prepared speech on informal occasions. Deliver a company statement to the press. Deal with questions.

Act as a host or be a guest at a meal or reception. Have reasonably wide "social" vocabulary. Can join in "social" conversation at parties and receptions. Can take part in "small talk".

Elicit information and advise in general terms on own specialist field.

STAGE E: TEACHERS' NOTES

General Note

By this stage the employee should have a fairly good understanding of how the language is used—i.e. what the communicative force of a particular structure is. The system of signalling devices built up in the last two stages can now be expanded. The employee can now be introduced to speech "gambits". A "gambit" is a subtler, more indirect signalling device which English speakers use, particularly in the course of discussion and arguments, to indicate that they are about to make a certain "move" in the game. From Stage E onwards, the employee can begin to grasp the significance of such "gambits", as, e.g. "I'm sure you're a better judge of this than I am, Charles, but don't you feel that we ought perhaps to . . . instead of . . . ?" He can begin to produce "gambits" in order to interrupt a speaker or raise an objection, without giving offence. At this stage he should be widening his vocabulary so that he can talk about other spheres of the business.

Language Specifications

New Grammar

Complex sentence forms
Devices for indicating the emphasis placed on a part of the utterance (e.g. *It was Per who said . . .*)

Old Grammar with New Usage

Present Continuous Tense with marker *Always* to indicate habit that amuses or irritates
Past time + *would* and *might* to indicate a more tentative or more formal approach
Present Perfect Continuous v. Present Perfect Simple/Past Simple (e.g. *We've been trying to work out how we can . . .* v. *We've tried to work out how we can . . .*)

New Communicative Acts

Reprimand using *You should/shouldn't have . . .* or *You were not authorised to . . .*

Urge someone using the emphatic *do* (e.g. *Do be careful what you say.*)
Express annoyance and irritation using phrases such as *Oh, for goodness sake, must you . . .* and by using marked intonation—e.g. a low rising tone

Extended Range of Communicative Acts

Value judgements using *could/was able to/managed to/succeeded in*
Release from obligation using *needn't*
Excusing oneself using *forgive me for . . .*

Making excuses using *We are not to blame for . . ./Owing to unforeseen . . ./ I've been meaning to . . .*
Making suggestions using *Shall we . . ./We'll . . ., shall we?*
Giving advice using *We (would) advise/recommend you to . . .*
Encouraging other people to talk using non-words (e.g. *mm, I see, yes, uhuh,*) + low rising tone
Giving warnings using *I must warn you that/not to . . .*
Issuing threats using (Reluctantly) *we shall be obliged to . . .*
Issuing invitations using *Would you care to . . .*
Expressing surprise using *Imagine/Fancy* + Gerund and *It's a wonder . . .*
Being sarcastic or joking using *It's a wonder*
Expressing exasperation using *Oh, for . . .'s sake*
Expressing dislikes with the verbs *can't stand/can't bear/loathe/* + Gerund
Making identification using *You must be . . .*
Expressing regret using the verbs *regret/apologise*
Expressing sympathy/commiseration using *How awful/awkward/embarrassing for you*
Expressing gratitude/relief using *I'm most grateful to you for . . ./It's a good thing . . .*

The Process of Exchanging Information

Report speech with a range of reporting verbs, i.e. *suggest, claim, advise, assure, promise, refuse,* etc.
Assert information and emphasise a point using the emphatic *do*
Confirm/check information received using the signal *Am I to understand . . .?* and *Now, let's just see if I've got this straight.*
Consult people using signal *What would you do in my position?*
Sound out other people's views using *I'd be interested to know/find out . . .*
Express agreement and support with signals *I'm in full agreement with . . ./I fully support . . .*
Dispute information received with the signal *I question* + Noun/*whether*
Full range of performative verbs to act as signallers, e.g. *I object to . . ./I deny . . ./I refuse to . . ./*etc.

Modality of the Information

Signal phrases: *I'm convinced/As I see it/D'you see/I can forsee/I presume/I anticipate/I suppose/This leads me to believe/I've no doubt/ By my reckoning/I suspect/You surely don't believe . . .*

Use of the verb *seem* and the adverb *likely* to indicate degree of certainty
Use of the verb phrase *I'd be willing to* . . . to indicate willingness
Use of the verb *consider* to indicate intention
Full range of verbs to act as signal, e.g. *promise/undertake/guarantee/offer/ compel/oblige/*etc.

Rational Organisation of the Information

Signal: *It follows that/it must be/it must have been* to indicate deduction
Use of *provided that/as long as/unless/given that* to indicate condition
Use of *otherwise/with the result that/* to indicate consequence
Signal: *. . . is defined us . . ./. . . May be said to . . .* to indicate definition/ classification
Signal: *As I see it . . .* to indicate interpretation
Use of *whilst/whereas* to indicate comparison
Use of *nevertheless* to indicate contrast
Signal: *In view of the fact that . . .* to indicate cause
Signal: *Furthermore/besides/what's more* to indicate additional information
Signal: *Assuming that . . ./Given that . . .* to indicate presupposition
Signal: *That is to say . . .* to indicate clarification
Signal: *In spite of the (fact that) . . ./Despite . . .* to indicate concession
Signal: *Bearing in mind that . . .* to remind

Lexis and Situation

Gradually moving away from the employee's own special sphere of responsibility to a wider range of business situations.

STAGE E: Reading and Writing

Employee should be able to:

Understand (and translate if required) details of regulations in familiar field. Understand intention of regulations in an unfamiliar field.

Understand, translate if necessary, and act on the majority of routine correspondence, even when in non-standard English as long as it is within employee's job area.

Understand (and translate if necessary) fairly straightforward abbreviated notes and messages (where message is not complex).

Understand (and translate if necessary) the information in a specification (e.g. Standards) together with main points of instruction. (Where item described is within own fields.)

Read at own speed non-standard reports in own and closely-related fields (and provide a translation if required). Identify information and assess need for further action.

Understand and complete accurately the majority of routine and non-standard forms likely to be encountered in connection with job, travel, personnel, etc.

Read at an acceptable speed (and translate if required) standard report in own or closely-related field. Extract information as basis for action.

Understand factual information in minutes of a meeting.

Understand most types of announcement (memo, notice, circular, etc.). Act on these where related to job area. Translate if required.

Understand (and translate if required) description of design, operation, construction, application, etc., when accompanied by diagrams and illustrations, and when product is familiar.

Understand (and translate broadly if required), a news item or informative article in a field within employee's knowledge/experience.

Compose short simple non-routine letters relating to facts or events. Prepare translations of similar letters in summary form.

Compose brief non-routine telex/telegrams. Write brief notes using short forms, abbreviations, etc.

Write a set of clear instructions or requests in the form of a passage. Translate these from and into English.

Write brief, simple factual articles for internal publication/circulation.

Write factual/informative memos, letters, etc., within own and related departments. Draft informative notices for circulation. Translate material for similar purposes.

The Stages of Attainment Scale is administered by means of a Test Battery. There are four tests, as shown on the diagram below

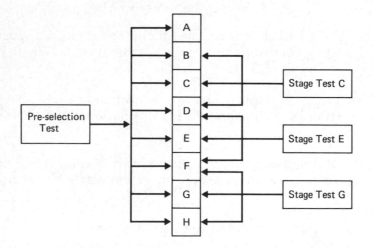

The Pre-Selection Test is designed primarily for establishing the existing level of language competence in relation to the Stages of Attainment Scale. It is therefore most frequently used by companies before training starts, the results given when set against the objective set showing the training gap that has to be filled.

It is also used by some companies simply to establish whether training is necessary at all; for recruitment purposes; and in one-off situations to decide whether a particular employee can safely be sent to an international meeting or not.

The three Stage Tests are designed for use at the end of the training period, and are far more detailed. Their purpose is to enable the company to assess whether the training objective has been met or not. They therefore act as a control mechanism for the training department over the effectiveness of their in-company training programme, and, indeed, over the quality of service offered by independent language schools, whether local or in this country.

The implications of this approach and use of a framework such as the Stages of Attainment Scale and its associated Test Battery are many. For the employer, the principal results are that he can set training objectives related to job requirements and, through the Test Battery, can assess the effectiveness of his training programme—not only in learning terms, but also in cost terms.

For the employee wishing to learn English for his job—and we must remember that, like his company, he may have no interest at all in the English language *per se*—it provides a means of ensuring that what he is asked to learn is the language he actually needs.

For the teacher, such an approach enables him to direct his teaching to what his students actually require. He and his language school are enabled to provide the training service for which both are, after all, being paid.

The Stages of Attainment Scale and its accompanying Test Battery therefore constitute a framework within which company language training can take place, and are practical tools within that framework for both management and the language teacher.

THE TEST OF ENGLISH FOR INTERNATIONAL COMMUNICATION (TOEIC)

PROTASE E. WOODFORD

Educational Testing Service, Princeton

Educational Testing Service in Princeton, New Jersey was founded in 1947. Prior to 1947, three major institutions: The College Entrance Examination Board, the Carnegie Foundation for the Advancement of Teaching and the American Council on Education had each, as non-profit educational agencies, carried out testing programs for schools, colleges and universities in the United States. In 1947 the three organizations founded a new, independent, non-profit organization dedicated to the development of programs and research in educational measurement and assessment. The new organization—Educational Testing Service (ETS)—has become the largest and most well-known educational measurement organization in the United States and perhaps in the world. Currently, there are over 2,000 full-time employees in Princeton and ten regional offices from Puerto Rico to California.

ETS experience in foreign language testing dates from the beginning of the organization. The College Board, one of the three parent organizations, had administered foreign language tests since the turn of the century. It is interesting to note that the foreign language tests changed very little between 1900 and 1960. Foreign language teaching stressed the development of reading skills only and the memorization of grammatical rules. Foreign language tests were limited to testing reading ability and the knowledge of grammatical rules.

In the 1960s the emphasis in foreign language teaching in the United States changed from reading and writing to understanding and speaking. The testing industry, always a few steps behind, began to find ways to measure these new skills.

For many years foreign language teachers taught something they called "language" but often had little to do with the ability to communicate with a speaker of the language being taught. We cannot blame the teachers because they themselves often lacked those same skills. Furthermore, it was rare that a student would ever actually find himself in a real life situation that required him to communicate in another language. And so language instruction and language testing existed in a vacuum, unaffected by the real world. Those few people who really had to learn French went to Paris for a few years, those who needed German, to Berlin, Russian, to the Soviet Union. I expect that a similar situation existed in other countries. But as you will see, the way in which we test can inform the manner in which we teach.

Consider a language as the language teachers and testers do, not as a single unit but in its four component parts or skills: Listening or understanding, speaking, reading and writing. Two of the skills are receptive or passive— reading and listening, and two are active, productive or creative; speaking and writing. The testing of passive skills has always been much more common than the testing of productive or active skills for a variety of reasons. One of the most important reasons is that passive or receptive skills can be measured by objective, machine-scorable tests. Productive skills testing always requires human judging and thus becomes more expensive, more time-consuming and less reliable. The Test of English as a Foreign Language (TOEFL) is administered to tens of thousands of students on the same day around the world. The books are sent to Princeton, New Jersey and the scores or marks are sent to the students within a few weeks. This is possible because the test is machine scorable. If a speaking test or a writing test were added and had to be rated by a person, it would most likely take months rather than weeks to report the scores and be much more expensive. The test, therefore, is limited to testing passive or receptive skills.

There are two words basic to the vocabulary of the test makers—reliability and validity. A test must be both valid and reliable if it is to serve any useful purpose. A reliable test is one that gives consistent results. If I take a mathematics test now and score 200 and take another version of the same test tomorrow without having learned any more mathematics, I should get 200 again. When we measure a kilometer of distance our kilometer always is 1000 meters long. If my kilometer is 800 meters and yours is 1100 meters, we do not have reliable measurement. Reliability then is the consistency of the measure. A test can be reliable, however, and not necessarily be valid. A test is valid if it tests what it is supposed to test. This seems obvious but many, many tests fail completely to test what they say they test. Nowhere is this more true than in the testing of foreign languages. You might know all the rules of Arabic grammar, the history of the Middle East and thus receive very high marks on an Arabic test. But if the test is supposed to indicate how well you speak Arabic and doesn't require you to speak Arabic, it is of doubtful validity. You might be mute and still do very well on such a test. You also would do well on the test if it were given to you a second or third time. The test would be a very reliable but invalid test of your ability to speak Arabic.

In addition to the questions of validity and reliability, there is the issue of interpretability. What does a score or mark mean? Those who have taken the

TOEFL know that 650 or 700 is a "good" score and "400" is "not so good". But what do we mean by "good" or "not good"? For tests like the TOEFL, the Graduate Management Admissions Test (GMAT) and others, a score or mark is a way to compare performance against that of a standard or reference population. The tests used for university admission have a scale from 200 to 800, a mean or average of 500. The standard deviation is 100. That means that about 68% of all scores fall between 400 and 600. Scores above 600 are "very good" and scores below 400 are "not good". The scores themselves, however, provide only one piece of information about an examinee. Universities that accept the examinee will follow their history. If most of the students who score over 550 and who have good secondary school records succeed at the university and those below 500 do not, then the university may set 550 as the minimum acceptable score. The kind of validity involved with university admissions tests is "predictive" validity. Do the tests predict student performance in the future at a university? Foreign language tests require a different kind of validity. We call it "concurrent" validity. If a language test is supposed to measure whether a person can read Japanese or not then the person who scores high on the test should be able to pick up the Japanese newspaper and tell us what the lead article says. The low scorer should not be able to do it.

To say that someone is in the top 10% of the group that took a test is not very informative if we don't know what that high scorer is capable of doing. We need a description of the tasks that can be accomplished by examinees at different score levels. This, to my knowledge, has rarely been done before.

The TOEIC is a multiple-choice test of English for non-native speakers of English. It consists of two sections: Listening Comprehension and Reading. There are one hundred questions in each section. In the Listening Section the examinee is required to listen to a variety of recorded English stimulus material and answer questions printed in English in the test book that are based on the recorded stimuli. In the Reading Section, the examinee is required to read a variety of passages of varying subject matter and of different lengths and levels of difficulty, and respond to questions based upon the content of the passages.

Separate scaled scores are provided for each section of the TOEIC. The part score scales range from 5 to 495. The total score is obtained by adding the two part scores thus providing for a total score scale ranging from 10 to 990.

What was proposed was a departure from the traditional academic testing of English grammar rules and literature. The challenge, as we saw it, was to develop highly valid and reliable measures of real-life reading and listening skills and, to the extent possible, indirect measures of speaking and writing. In addition, and this is the most exciting part of the project, we were to develop a procedure for score interpretation that would allow score recipients to actually *see* the kind of English that the examinees at different score levels could read and to *see* also, typical samples of the examinees' writing efforts, in English, for different score levels. Score recipients would also be provided with samples of English speech by examinees at different levels. For many years programs such as TOEFL have attempted to develop such a system for score interpretation. To develop such a system with examinees from hundreds of different language backgrounds is a monumental job. Separate materials would have to be created for speakers of Spanish, Chinese, Japanese, French, etc. because we know that the kinds of native language interference are different for each group. Now, however, with a monolingual examinee population, the development of interpretive materials with performance samples became feasible.

The TOEIC was designed to meet the need for a measure of English language skills outside of the traditional academic context. What was sought was the development of highly valid and reliable direct measures of real-life reading and listening skills. It was hoped that the TOEIC would also provide, indirectly, an indication of an examinee's ability to write and speak English as well.

The final test specifications called for 100 items or questions in listening comprehension and 100 in reading comprehension as follows:

Listening Comprehension

Part I	One Picture, Four Spoken Sentences	20 items
Part II	Spoken Utterances, Three Spoken Responses	30 items
Part III	Short Conversation, Four printed answers	30 items
Part IV	Short talks, four printed questions and answers	20 items
		100 items

Reading Comprehension

Part V	Incomplete Sentences	40 items
Part VI	Error Recognition—Underlines	20 items
Part VII	Reading Comprehension—Passages	40 items
		100 items

The first form of TOEIC was administered in Japan on December 2, 1979. 2710 examinees were included in the sample upon which the analysis is based.

On the basis of the preliminary item analysis two items from Part IV and one item each from Parts VI and VII were deleted from the final scoring of the test. Therefore, the raw scores for each section of the test were based on 98 items, 98 for listening comprehension and 98 for reading, or a total of 196 scorable items out of the 200 in the full examination. The scores that were reported were not raw scores, they were converted scores.

The raw scores on every form of TOEIC will be converted to the common scale established at the first administration. For each of the two sections, the scale was set to range from 5 to 495. The Total Score is the sum of the converted scores for the two sections. Thus, the range of possible Total Scores is 10 to 990. A statistical procedure called "score equating" will be used to determine the appropriate conversion formula for each new form so that a given converted score (e.g. 640) will represent the same level of ability regardless of the form taken or the ability level of the group with whom it was taken.

It is important to note that the total score is not *directly* related to the total number of correct answers. Subsequent forms of the TOEIC have been equated through section scores and not from total score to total score.

The examinee group who sat for the TOEIC in December 1979 contained an unexpectedly large proportion of persons who were *not* affiliated with companies. For this reason separate raw score statistics were obtained for each group.

Table A. Raw Score Data

(Based on 98 items listening, 98 items reading)

	Company affiliated	Unaffiliated
Number of persons	828	1,884
Listening comprehension		
Mean score	56.98	62.55
Standard deviation	14.42	13.75
Reading comprehension		
Mean score	64.97	69.75
Standard deviation	15.69	13.72
Correlation between listening comp., reading comp.	0.80	0.74

It should also be noted that because an examinee's listening comprehension and reading comprehension scores could be compared to each other, the section scores were scaled in such a way that the means and the standard deviations for the two sections are equal. An important result of this procedure is that the two sections have equal weight or importance in the total score.

Is the Test Appropriate for the Examinees?

Middle difficulty is defined as the midpoint between the expected chance score—the score that would be expected if every item were answered at random—and the maximum possible score. Middle difficulty for the TOEIC listening comprehension section, consisting of 30 three-choice and 68 four-choice items would be a score of 62.5.

Therefore, the listening comprehension section for the "affiliated" group was somewhat harder than middle difficulty since the mean score for that group was 56.98. However, the listening section was almost exactly at middle difficulty for the "unaffiliated" group whose mean score was 62.55.

The reading comprehension section was easier than middle difficulty (61.25) for both the "affiliated" and the "unaffiliated" groups whose mean scores were 64.97 and 69.75 respectively.

Table A shows that the raw score for listening comprehension section was 21 to 98 (of 98). The range for the reading section was 17 to 96 (of 98).

Of the 20 items in Part I—one picture four spoken choices, the mean score for the 2,710 examinees in the sample was 16.44 or a mean of 82% of the total possible score.

Part II (Question and three spoken responses) was slightly harder than middle difficulty (20) for three-choice items. Parts III and IV (short conversations and short talks) were the two most difficult parts of the test

The most difficult part in the reading section was Part VI (error recognition) which was slightly harder than middle difficulty. Parts V and VII (incomplete sentences and reading comprehension passages) were relatively easy.

The parts of the test arranged in order of increasing difficulty are I (easiest), VII, V, VI, II, IV, III (hardest).

Reliabilities (Kuder Richardson Formula 20)

The reliability of the listening comprehension section was 0.916 and the standard error of measurement in scaled score units was 25.95.

For the reading section, the reliability was 0.930 and the standard error was 23.38.

Total test reliability was estimated at 0.956 and the standard error was 34.93.

These reliabilities are well within the generally accepted limits for measurement of individual achievement.

Correlation Between the Two Sections—Listening and Reading

The correlation between the sections was 0.769 for the analysis sample. This would indicate that each score provides somewhat different information about the examinee and justifies reporting separate scores.

Is the test too long or too short for the time available to the examinee?

Because the listening section of the test is timed and paced by the tape recording, it is assumed that all the examinees finish the section. Eighty-seven per cent of the examinees in the sample completed the reading comprehension section of the test and 99.5% completed three-quarters of the test.

It is also interesting to note that the average number of questions not answered was less than one for listening comprehension and less than two for reading comprehension.

These data indicate that speed was not an important factor for either section of the test.

How difficult was the test for the Population?
The average percent correct for the items in the listening comprehension section was 62%.
The average percent correct for the items in the reading section was 70%.
How well do the test questions discriminate?
The criterion used for each item is the section of the test in which the item appears. The mean biserial correlation for the listening section was 0.45.
The mean biserial correlation for the reading section was 0.49.

The Scale

The TOEIC scale has a range from 5 to 495 for each section.

For the Listening Comprehension section the observed range—the scores actually obtained by the examinees—went from a low of 40 to a high of 495. The mean scaled score was 290.

The observed range of scaled scores for the reading section was from a low of 5 to a high of 455. The mean scaled score was 288. (No *real* score of 288 exists since all scores are reported in multiples of 5. A 288 score would be reported as 290.)

As shown in Table A, most of the scores on the listening section fall between 200 and 370. Approximately 68% of the scores fall within that range.

For the reading section most scores fall between 210 and 385. Approximately 70% of the scores fall within that range.

The total score for TOEIC is the sum of the two section scores as was mentioned earlier. The mean total scaled score was 578. Most total scores fall between 400 and 745. Sixty-eight percent—approximately—of the examinees' scores were within that range.

It is quite gratifying to note that the scale functions as intended. Almost all points on the scale are utilized for both sections of the test as well as for the total score.

Results of TOEIC Validity Study

Subsequent to the first administration of the Test of English for International Communication on December 2, 1979, a series of validation exercises were carried out in Japan to determine the degree to which performance on the TOEIC corresponded to performance on more direct measures of each of four language skills: Listening Comprehension, Reading, Writing and Speaking. In addition a version of the Test of English as a Foreign Language (TOEFL) was administered to a sample of TOEIC examinees in order to determine the relationship of performance on one measure to performance on the other.

When score distributions were obtained for the first administration of the TOEIC, 500 examinees were selected to take the TOEFL. The 500 were selected on the basis of their scores on the TOEIC. One hundred examinees were selected at each of five approximate score levels: 950, 765, 580, 315, 45. A smaller group of 20 examinees from each group of 100 was selected. To these examinees a series of direct measures of language ability were administered.

The Direct Measures were as follows:

Listening Comprehension

Twenty-five taped English stimuli consisting of 15 short statements or questions and 10 dialogues were played to the examinees. For each of the twenty-five exercises there were three questions to be answered by the examinees. The questions were asked in Japanese by a Japanese examiner and the examinees were encouraged to answer in Japanese. There was a total of 75 scorable items on the Direct Measure of Listening Comprehension.

Reading Comprehension

Reading tasks in English of many kinds were presented to the examinees. Some exercises consisted of a single English word as it might appear on a label or a sign. Other exercises required the examinee to read a table of contents in a catalog in order to find a particular product; or to understand a piece of advertising copy. Examinees were provided ample time to read each selection. When an examinee had completed reading the selection, an examiner would ask questions, in Japanese, about the content of the selection. There were 30 content questions in the Direct Measure of Reading. The examinees answered the questions, orally, in Japanese.

Writing

There were three parts, each with a different kind of exercise included in the Direct Measure of Writing. The first part consisted of 10 "dehydrated sentences". The "dehydrated sentences" were sentence elements from which the examinee was to produce a coherent English sentence making any necessary changes or additions, for example: employees/receive/raise/next year → The employees will receive a raise next year. Fifteen minutes were allowed for Part I.

In the second part the examinee was required to write a 25–40 word letter to a manufacturer complaining about the manufacturer's delay in shipping an order to him or to her. Examinees were given twenty minutes in which to write the letter. In the third part of the Direct Measure of Writing, the examinee was asked to write the English translation of ten Japanese sentences. The sentences were chosen because they contained specific structural and lexical problems.

Possible scores on Part I ranged from 0 to 50. Possible scores on Part II ranged from 0 to 14. Possible scores on Part III ranged from 0 to 75.

A composite direct measure of English language writing skill was created from the three direct measure exercises. This was done to create a single score that would reflect the various components of writing skill in a reliable way. Scores from the three exercises were made comparable by the process of standardization. Each person's score on each exercise was transformed by subtracting the group's mean score on the exercise from the person's score, and dividing by the group's standard deviation. This score was multiplied by 10 and added to 50. In this way each exercise was placed on a scale with a mean of 50 and a standard deviation of 10. Based on an analysis of the writing tasks, it was decided to differentially weight the three tasks. The following table gives the means, standard deviations, and weights for the three tasks:

Task	Mean	Standard Deviation	Weight
Dehydrated sentences	37.824	7.243	0.3
Business letter	5.859	3.211	0.5
Sentence Translation	64.033	9.406	0.2

The range for the composite score for the Direct Measure of Writing was 12–70.

Speaking

The Direct Measure of Speaking Ability was the Language Proficiency Interview (LPI) used by the U.S. Department of State, the Peace Corps and various state and local government agencies. The LPI is a face-to-face interview procedure. Examinees are rated on a 0–5 scale with plus values for all ratings from 0 through 4. For this study interviewers in Japan who were native speakers of English and who were experienced linguists or language instructors were trained by ETS staff to conduct the LPI. Each interview was recorded and the recording sent to ETS Princeton where it was rated by an experienced ETS rater.

Results

The examinees who underwent the direct measures were divided into five groups for purposes of analysis. Examinees were grouped according to their part scores on the TOEIC. For both Listening and Reading, Group I had TOEIC part scores below or equal to 100; Group II had TOEIC part scores between 100 and 205; Group III had TOEIC part scores between 205 and 300; Group IV, between 305 and 400 and Group V, 405 or above.

Listening

Ninety-nine examinees were included in the sample that took the Direct Listening exercises. The total possible score was 75. The mean scores for each group are as follows:

Group I	(TOEIC Listening part scores equal to or less than 100)	15.4 (of 75)
Group II	(TOEIC Listening part scores between 105–200)	23.4 (of 75)
Group III	(TOEIC Listening part scores between 205–300)	45.0 (of 75)
Group IV	(TOEIC Listening part scores between 305–400)	56.4 (of 75)
Group V	(TOEIC Listening part scores above 400)	65.6 (of 75)

The two listening measures correlate very highly—0.90. The TOEIC Listening Section has a multiple choice format. The examinee must *read* the answer choices in English. For that reason, the TOEIC Listening Section is not a "pure" test of listening ability. The results of the study indicate that the Listening Section of TOEIC is indeed an accurate indicator of an examinee's ability to comprehend spoken English.

Reading Comprehension

A total of 99 examinees were administered the Direct Reading Measures. The total possible score was 30. The mean scores for each group are as follows:

Group I	(TOEIC Reading part scores equal to or less than 100)	10.0 (of 30)
Group II	(TOEIC Reading part scores between 105–200)	17.6 (of 30)
Group III	(TOEIC Reading part scores between 205–300)	22.6 (of 30)
Group IV	(TOEIC Reading part scores betwen 305–400)	24.1 (of 30)
Group V	(TOEIC Reading part scores above 400)	26.8 (of 30)

Examinees were required to read English language material and answer questions in Japanese posed by Japanese examiners. The TOEIC Reading Test is in a multiple choice format. The examinee reads a question in English based on the content of the selection and chooses the one of four printed English options that he or she considers to be the best answer to the question.

The high degree of similarity of performance by the examinees on both the TOEIC Reading section and the Direct Measure of Reading suggest that the

TOEIC Reading Test provides a good indication of the examinee's ability to read English with understanding. The correlation between the two reading measures is 0.79.

Speaking

The level of agreement between TOEIC Listening part scores and the ratings for the Language Proficiency Interview is very high. There were 100 examinees included in the sample to whom the interview (LPI) was administered. The highest possible rating that could be achieved was a 5.0. The mean LPI ratings for each group are as follows:

Group I	(TOEIC Listening part scores equal to or less than 100)	0+ (0.76 of 5.0)
Group II	(TOEIC Listening part scores between 105–200)	1 (1.16 of 5.0)
Group III	(TOEIC Listening part scores between 205–300)	2 (1.99 of 5.0)
Group IV	(TOEIC Listening part scores between 305–400)	2+ (2.66 of 5.0)
Group V	(TOEIC Listening part scores above 400)	3+ (3.53 of 5.0)

A "plus" is recorded as 0.7.

The correlation between the TOEIC listening part score and the direct Language Proficiency Interview is 0.83. This high degree of correlation would seem to indicate that the TOEIC part score is a good predictor of the candidates' abilities to speak English even though the objective measure tests a receptive oral skill while the direct speaking measure tests a productive oral skill.

Writing

Three hundred and six examinees were included in the sample that took the direct writing exercises. The total possible weighted composite score was 70. The mean scores for each group are as follows:

Group I	(TOEIC Reading part scores equal to or less than 100)	23.8 (of 70)
Group II	(TOEIC Reading part scores between 105–200)	33.8 (of 70)
Group III	(TOEIC Reading part scores between 205–300)	46.0 (of 70)
Group IV	(TOEIC Reading part scores between 305–400)	50.9 (of 70)
Group V	(TOEIC Reading part scores above 400)	57.2 (of 70)

The direct writing measures correlated 0.83 with the TOEIC reading part score. This high correlation suggests that the TOEIC reading score is a good indication of the examinee's ability to write in English. It should be noted that the reading section of TOEIC contains questions that relate both to reading and to writing. Since these two component parts correlate highly with each other, as well as with the direct measures in writing and reading, a separate part score for writing is not necessary.

TOEFL

A total of 187 examiners were administered both TOEFL and TOEIC. Average TOEFL listening scores are presented for the five groups based on TOEIC Listening Comprehension score.

Group I	(TOEIC Listening part scores equal to or less than 100)	40.0
Group II	(TOEIC Listening part scores between 105–200)	41.9
Group III	(TOEIC Listening part scores between 205–300)	48.9
Group IV	(TOEIC Listening part scores between 305–400	54.7
Group V	(TOEIC Listening part scores above 400)	59.6

Likewise, average TOEFL Reading Comprehension scores are presented for the five groups based on TOEIC Listening Comprehension score.

Group I	(TOEIC Reading part scores equal to or less than 100)	34.7
Group II	(TOEIC Reading part scores between 105–200)	43.1
Group III	(TOEIC Reading part scores between 205–300)	48.0
Group IV	(TOEIC Reading part scores between 305–400)	54.3
Group V	(TOEIC Reading part scores above 400)	60.2

Conclusion

It can be concluded from an analysis of the data that TOEIC provides a good indication of candidates' language abilities in English. The Listening Comprehension part score of TOEIC correlates very highly with other measures of both listening and speaking. The TOEIC Reading part score correlates highly with other measures of candidates' abilities in both reading and writing. Although the mean scores of all the direct measures show a consistent relationship with the appropriate TOEIC part scores, it should be remembered that a standard error of measurement is inherent in all the measures in this study. Therefore, not all candidates scoring high or low on one measure will necessarily score equally high or low on another measure.

INTERNATIONAL COMMUNICATION THROUGH NON-NATIVE VARIETIES OF ENGLISH: THE CASE OF INDIAN ENGLISH

RAJA RAM MEHROTRA

Benares Hindu University

The emergence of non-native second language varieties of English particularly in the Commonwealth countries of Asia and Africa poses a serious problem in serving as a medium of international communication and understanding besides its implications in the field of learning and teaching the language. A case in point is English as spoken and written in India, usually labelled as Indian English (IE) which is said to be the "most widespread dialect on earth" spoken not only in India but the entire South-East Asia, East Africa, the Caribbean and Fiji (King, 1971: 2).

Way back in 1882 a reporter of *The Times* (London) remarked that a "thoughtful Englishman" would think of Indian writing in English in the same fashion as "Cicero would probably think of much of the Ciceronian Latin that is written at our schools and universities" (*The Times*, 1882: 8). Such an attitude is in fact noticeable in respect of all non-native varieties of English as is evident from the general statement made in the British Council Annual Report 1960–1961:

> In becoming a world language, English, some say, like any other common currency runs the risk of becoming worn, debased and subject to counterfeit. Its stamp is no longer authentic, it loses its clarity; it may become unrecognizeble (quoted in Sheshadri 1965: 17).

Ironically enough what to some appears to be worn, debased and counterfeit currency has taken on a new stamp, fresh authenticity and far greater circulation in the world at large than the so-called standard and unadulterated form. The concept of a standard form patronized by a small minority, however powerful, is not acceptable to the modern mind.

> The modern mind insists on having the process of standardization take the form of a democratic rather than an aristocratic process (Sapir, 1931).

What is needed therefore is change of attitude. The narrow parochial outlook thriving on built-in colour bar should be abandoned in favour of the one which is broad, catholic, cosmopolitan. Mark Twain has rightly reacted to such snobbish pretensions in these words,

> The King's English is not the king's. It is a joint stock company (quoted in Moss, 1973: XIII).

Similar is the import of a timely warning given in an editorial note in *The Times Literary Supplement*,

> English itself is a shared language in which we have no special proprietorial rights; all that matters ultimately is who can use it best . . . it is not reserved like a private telephone line exclusively for messages from England or even from America, but is a means of communication for all. We must learn to look outwards or die (*Times Literary Supplement* 1962: 591).

Thus Indian English is now an efficient and fairly stable variety existing in its own right, having its own frame of reference and symbolizing a distinct socio-cultural reality. In spite of the models set by the BBC and Voice of America IE could not but develop on lines of its own, independent of the mother tradition. The process of Indianization of the English language got a fresh boost after the departure of the native speakers from the Indian scene in 1947. English, it may be asserted, enjoys a special privilege in India. No other language in this country has been asked to do so many things in so many situations and at places so remote from one another both geographically and culturally. It is a truism that English tends to admit of greater variety and move in more diverse situations in a non-native multilingual setting than in its native surroundings. The number of second language speakers of English has constantly been on the increase and this has also contributed to its rich variation.

Intelligibility

IE often poses a problem of intercomprehensibility. It is generally believed that dialects are mutually intelligible and hence IE should be intelligible to the speakers of all other varieties of English. This is not always the case. There is a great deal in IE, particularly at the phonological and lexical levels, which is incomprehensible in varying degrees to the speakers of English outside the Indian subcontinent. At times English spoken in one part of the Indian territory is not correctly understood in the other part. The criterion of mutual intelligibility therefore is not an absolute fact and should admit a range of wide variations. As Robins points out,

> Mutual intelligibility, however, is not an all-or-none matter and admits of degrees from almost complete and unhindered comprehension to nearly total incomprehension without special training. (Robins, 1966: 59).

Postulating a cline of respectability seems inevitable in a situation like this.

It is common knowledge that the educated native speakers of English whether from England, U.S., Canada or Australia have no difficulty in understanding each other. Elaborating this phenomenon Prator says,

They (the mother tongue types of English) have sprung from a common linguistic stock and have evolved at a relatively slow rate over the decades since they achieved their separate identities. Such changes as have occurred in them have been largely the result of little understood processes of internal evolution and have kept pace with other elements of social change; even after many years of semi-independent development these types of English are still characterized by a high degree of intercomprehensibility, especially as spoken by the well-educated (Prator, 1968: 163).

Mutual intelligibility among the native varieties is due to the fact that they use the same grammatical structures, share a more or less similar lexicon, have recognizable ranges of phonemic contrasts and use similar patterns of stress and rhythm.

The position is, however, different with speakers of non-native second language varieties of English. For the purposes of intelligibility the situation in countries where English is used as a second language has been represented as a pyramid. The uppermost section of this pyramid is said to be suggestive of internationally comprehensible English, the middle indicating a local standard intelligible all over the country and the lowest being representative of pidgin which lacks intercomprehensibility (King, 1971: 3). This analogy cannot be applied to India for two reasons. Firstly, the situation in this country from this standpoint divides itself into four sections, instead of three, namely, the international, national, regional and pidgin or local. Secondly, the design of a pyramid does not fit in the Indian situation where the highest and the lowest points representing the international variety and pidgin are used by numerically small sections of population.

Let us illustrate here the four levels of intelligibility in the case of IE. There are certain items which are intelligible only locally. One such item is "Lanketing" which means visiting Lanka, a shopping centre near Benares University. The Indian pidgin English is also at times unintelligible as when the illiterate boatman talking to a foreign tourist pronounces "no" as "now" in the sentence "I 'now' burn the children" implying "I (we) don't burn the (dead) children."

Then there are certain lexical items which are intelligible only at the regional or state level. In most parts of South India the word "vessel" means "utensils". "Vessel" is nowhere used in this sense in any part of North India. The husband or wife's sister is called "co-brother" in Karnataka and Tamilnadu while "co-brother-in-law" in Andhra. These terms are also unknown in North India. The term "outbooks" meaning books outside the prescribed course is very common in West Bengal but unknown in the rest of the country. Similarly, the fictional writings of Kushwant Singh and Mulk Raj Anand often create difficulty in understanding among non-Punjabi speakers on account of the pull of the regional language in them.

The regional variations in English speech also hamper intelligibility. A Bengali speaker once annoyed his Punjabi neighbour by his inquiry, "Do you have T.B.?" At a Gujarati wedding recently an announcement was heard from the microphone, "The snakes are in the hole." It created panic among the guests. "Which hole?" was the unspoken hysteric question. There was a scramble for exit until someone clarified that the message was "The snacks are in the hall." It is evident from the foregoing that sometimes English used in one linguistic region in India is not understood in the other regions or by other mother-tongue groups in the same country.

We shall now pass on to the international intelligibility of IE. Excepting a small minority of Indians educated abroad,[2] most speakers of English in India are not easily and correctly understood overseas. There have been numerous complaints to this effect. Stocqueler as early as 1848 refers to the puzzling incomprehensibility of the English conversation in India which "wears strange suits" (Stocqueler, 1848: iii). King calls it a dangerous situation when the native speakers of English find it possible "to hear, and not understand speakers of English from the Indian sub-continent" (King, 1971: 2). Quirk also speaks of "that admittedly foreign sounding English of the Indians" who are studying in his country (Quirk, 1972: 48). It is feared that English in the Indian sub-continent and most African countries may, in the not very distant future, be found disintegrating into quite incomprehensible dialects. "If action is not taken," King warns "English is going to diverge into a series of Germanic languages as Latin did into the Romance languages" (King, 1971: 2). I wonder if it is possible, or even desirable to take any "action" at any level to compel or persuade these non-native varieties to conform to the standard native model. The inevitable fact seems to be that the more widely English spreads in a country, the more internationally incomprehensible it becomes.

What is it in IE that prevents its intelligibility abroad? One of the major hurdles is its phonological features making it distinct from the standard British variety. The vowel and consonant systems of IE are not identical with those in R.P. (Bansal, 1976). Among other phonological features of IE causing difficulty in the international intelligibility, mention may be made of difficulty with some consonant clusters resulting in deletion of one of the consonants, substitution of some R.P. diphthongs by monothongs, confusion between long and short vowels, a strong tendency for retroflexion, incorrect accentuation, neglect of weak forms and the absence of characteristic English rhythm and intonation (Bansal, 1976; Masica, 1966). At the phonological level one perceives several kinds of Indian English, each one showing unmistakably its allegiance to a regional language whose phonetic features influence it. Thus one can speak, among other, of Tamil English, Bengali English, Punjabi English, Hindi English or "Hinglish" and so on. This has well been demonstrated by a reader in a letter to the editor of *The Illustrated Weekly of India*:

> *Tamil English*
> "Eye yate yeleven yeggs" (I ate eleven eggs).
> "Meester Bharma uaj bhomitting in the bharandah, Sir!" (Mr. Verma was vomitting in the Varandah, Sir!)

Hindi English
  "It ij terribull. Prejence is poor in i-school." (It is terrible, presence is poor in school.)
Punjabi English
  "Go sutterait in the suttereet and ju bill find the house ju bant!" (Go straight in this street and you will find the house you want!) (Sharma, 1974: 6).

At the lexical level intelligibility is hampered by interpolation of words from Indian languages, hybrid-formations and neologisms. Besides a large number of Indian words that figure in Indian English writing (Yule and Burnell 1903, Rao 1954, Kachru 1973 and 1975) posing threat to intelligibility, some common English words are given new extra-dictionary meanings not to be found in the varieties of English outside the Indian subcontinent. One of the meanings of the word "boy" in IE is a male servant or a bearer in a hotel as in the sentence, "Boy! Get me some toast." This meaning is non-existent in British English. The term "four-twenty" meaning a "cheat" or "swindler" in IE is absolutely unknown outside the country. The word "source" is often used in IE in the sense of "influence, particularly of a resourceful person." "Source" in this sense is not used in British English. In the sentence "What are the subjects that you offered at B.A.?", "offer" is used in the sense of "take" which is not to be found in English dictionaries and the British usage. Similarly, colony, family, tempo, compound, division, moderator and weightage are some other words which have special meaning in IE usage.

Quite a few lexical items in IE are the result of hybrid formation, i.e. lathi-charge, bhabi-hood, coolidom, motor-gari, double roti. Often such formations are in the nature of fixed collocation and are bound by what Kachru calls "structural constraints" (Kachru, 1975: 63).

Even more interesting is the way in which Hindi words are made to behave with English inflexional endings added to them. Look at the following illustrations drawn from the private letters of some university students in India:

  I *lagaoed* a lot of pull.
  I *phiraoed* a couple of girls in the bazaar.
  Have you been able to *patao* that girl?
  You must *maro* at least 80% marks if you want a good job.
  Mr. Gupta was *gheraoed* for two hours last evening.

Some other examples of this type are *salammed*, *kukru kruing*, *dhotied* blackman. An example of the kind given by Goffin is,

  "The engine does not *chal* properly" (Goffin, 1934: 21).

Of particular relevance in this context is the extension of semantic features of the English lexical items. Notice for instance, the following sentences, all drawn from the domain of education, which in a recent survey—conducted by me—have been found to be perfectly intelligible on pan-Indian basis but at the same time absolutely unintelligible to the educated native speakers of English in Britain. The special meaning in IE usage is given within brackets:

After abusing me he left saying he would *see* me outside the college. (He would beat me when he finds me outside the college).
I came here by a *tempo*. (tempo—a three wheeled power-driven vehicle larger than auto-rickshaw).
I bought a dozen *copies* for my daughter. (copies—exercise books).
He has been appointed *moderator* for the B.A. examination. (moderator—a subject expert who scrutinizes the question papers set for an examination before they are sent to the press).
This year there was no *mass-cut* in the college. (mass-cut—boycott *en masse*).

It is important to note that the cases of total incomprehensibility such as these are in no way attributable to the cultural differences. Similar illustrations can be had from the other domains in IE and this in effect belies the popular belief that cultural gap is the only factor causing incomprehensibility of IE.

Another interesting fact that emerged out of this survey is that there are numerous items in IE that were found to be intelligible to some native speakers while unintelligible to others within the same country, viz. England. For instance, when asked to explain what they understood by the IE expression "Her face-cut is very impressive," some native speakers of English gave the correct response scoring 100% intelligibility, i.e. "Her profile is impressive" or "The shape of her face is very attractive," while others failed to understand the sentence correctly and came out with a variety of interpretations, some of them rather amusing: "She has good bones," "Her hair-cut is very impressive," "Her facial scar is very striking," "She cut her face badly, poor girl," "Sounds as though she has been in a fight with the knives out," "Does the girl shave?" The question of international intelligibility of IE and in fact the other non-native varieties of English is no simple matter and calls for a good deal of caution in its handling.

Before winding up our discussion on this subject, it may be asserted that only a small fraction of the Indian population, consisting mostly of academics, scientists, diplomats, top industrialists and business executives, is bothered about the intelligibility at the international level. What primarily concerns the majority of the speakers of English in India is comprehensibility of their speech and writing on pan-Indian basis which in effect stresses the need for evolving what R. H. Robins said recently in a personal interview to the present author "One standard for the whole subcontinent." There is no denying the fact that it is much more important to understand one's own countrymen than to understand outsiders.

A related issue is that of acceptability. Intelligibility and acceptability do not always go together. An utterance may be perfectly intelligible but not at all acceptable. For instance, the following IE expressions have in the course of my survey been found to be 100% intelligible to the native speakers of English in Britain but at the same time totally unacceptable to them. They would never use these sentences themselves.

I would like to have bed tea everyday.
The warden reached in time and cooled the matter.

You cannot get a good job without some source.
Please inform the staff concerned to do the needful.
He speaks chaste Urdu.
He passed the examination in the second division.
May I know your good name, please?

Often the native speakers themselves are not unanimous in their judgement on acceptability of IE item. Forty native-speakers of English in Great Britain were asked by me in a questionnaire if the following sentence, commonly heard in all parts of India, would be acceptable to them: "What subjects have you offered for your B.A. degree?" It was acceptable to 16, unacceptable to 24. Similar reactions were received in respect of the majority of IE samples. Look at the range of comments they have made on another common IE sentence. "I hope this finds you in the pink of health." Some of these overtly contradict one another: "unacceptable," "not best English," "out of date," "pedantic," "stilted," "vulgar," "antiquated," "slightly archaic," "a non-U expression," "very upper class," "acceptable," "a cast-iron idiom."

This leads us to the inevitable conclusion that we have to develop our own norms of acceptability instead of seeking every now and then the opinion of the native speaker who, as we have seen above, are not unanimous in their pronouncements. The English used in India cannot but take its mould from the contextual spectrum of its speakers—their life style, their thought-ways, and the very ethos they breathe. The norms of acceptability change from place to place, time to time. In this connection we cannot but admire the approach of an Edinburgh teacher who when asked to comment on an IE item in course of my survey remarked, "I would not say it myself, but I would accept someone else saying it." Here is an attitude in the right direction. Then, there are expressions which are neither fully acceptable nor fully unacceptable but can be shown at various points between the two extremes on the cline of acceptability in accordance with their role "towards the maintenance of appropriate patterns of life" (Firth, 1957: 225). As Greenbaum tersely remarked,

> Whether a form is acceptable is not a question that can be answered simply. We have also to ask such questions as who finds it acceptable and in what contexts (Greenbaum, 1975: 171).

NOTES

1. Cf. J. R. Firth, "It is impossible to transfer a language 6000 miles overseas and expect it to remain as it was or to develop it on the lines of the mother country" (Firth, 1964: 197).
2. This includes men like Jawahar Lal Nehru, Nirad Chaudry, C. D. Deshmukh and Sham Lal, a former editor of *The Times of India* who all possess what Bloomfield calls a "native-like control" of the English language (Bloomfield, 1935: 56). Quirk, for instance, pays compliments to Nehru's command over English in these words, "And at the top of the scale we get a man like Mr. Nehru, speaking an English perfectly comprehensible and acceptable throughout the English speaking world (Quirk, 1972: 49). Writers like R. K. Narain and Raja Rao have already crossed the national frontiers without difficulty and opposition. Iyengar is not exaggerating when he says, "At its best Indian writing in English compares not unfavourably with the best writing in Australia, Canada or even in the United States

and England" (Iyengar, 1961: 140). Among earlier masters of English in India we may mention C. R. Das, C. Y. Chintamani, Shiva Swami Aiyar and Brijendra Nath Seal. The tradition of Indian writers of good English is more than a century old. One of the issues of *The Times* (London) published in 1882 has this to say in an editorial note, "A considerable portion of the English Press in India is written by natives; and many of these so-called 'Anglo-Native' papers are written with great ability and in excellent idiomatic English" (*Times*, 1882: 8). Thus there has always been in India a galaxy of writers and speakers whose English was neutral, near-native and autonomous.

REFERENCES

BANSAL, R. K. (1976) *The Intelligibility of Indian English* Monograph No. 4. Hyderabad: Central Institute of English and Foreign Languages.

BLOOMFIELD, L. (1935, 1963) *Language*. Delhi: Motilal Banarsi Dass.

FIRTH, J. R. (1957) "General Linguistics and Descriptive Grammar," *Paper in Linguistics 1934–1951*. London: OUP.

FIRTH, J. R. (1964) "Speech", *The Tongues of Men and Speech*. London: OUP.

GOFFIN, R. C. (1934) Some Notes on Indian English. In S.P.E. Tract no. XLI. Oxford.

GREENBAUM, S. (1975) "Language Variation and Acceptability," *TESOL Quarterly*, **9**, 2. June.

IYENGAR, K. R. S. (1961) "The Literature of India." In Mcleod, A. L. (ed.), *The Commonwealth Press*. New York.

KACHRU, B. B. (1973) "Toward a Lexicon of Indian English," Kahane, L. (ed.), *Issues in Linguistics*. Urbana.

KACHRU, B. B. (1975) Lexical innovations in South Asian English, *International Journal of the Sociology of Language*, **4**. The Hague: Mouton.

KING, A. H. (1971) "Intercomprehensibility—the Humpty Dumpty Problem of English as a World Language," *The Incorporated Linguist*, **11**, 1, January.

MASICA, C. P. (1966) "The Sound System of General Indian English." Mimeographed. Hyderabad: CIEFL.

MOSS, N. (1973) *What's the Difference*? London.

PRATOR, C. (1968) "The British Heresy in TESL." In Fishman, J. *et al.*, *Language Problems of Developing Nations*. New York, Wiley.

QUIRK, R. (1972) *The English Language and the Images of Matter*. London: OUP.

RAO, G. S. (1954) *Indian Words in English*. Oxford: At the Clarendon Press.

ROBINS, R. H. (1966) *General Linguistics: An Introductory Survey*. London: Longmans.

SAPIR, R. P. (1974) "Desi English," *The Illustrated Weekly of India*, March, **31**.

SHESHADRI, C. K. (1965) "British English and Indian English: A Linguistic Comparison," *Journal of the M.S. University of Baroda* (Humanities Number) XIV, April.

STOCQUELER, J. H. (1848) *The Oriental Interpreter and Treasury of the East India Knowledge: A Companion to "The Handbook of British India."* London.

The Times (1882) "Baboo English." April 11, London.

The Times Literary Supplement (1962) "In Common" (Editorial). August 10.

YULE, H. and BURNELL, A. C. (1903) Hobson-Jobson. London.

3. Research

THE INTERNATIONAL USES OF ENGLISH: RESEARCH IN
PROGRESS

VERNER BICKLEY

East-West Culture Learning Institute, Honolulu, Hawaii

Introduction

This paper is a report on language research in progress at the Culture Learning Institute of the East-West Center, an educational in-
stitution established in Honolulu, Hawaii, in 1960 by United States'
Congressional legislation and now operated as a quasi-public, educational, non-profit corporation with an independent Board of
Governors who, at present, come from Fiji, India, Japan, the
Philippines, Singapore and the United States.

In co-operation with a number of scholars and other professionals from different countries, cultures and disciplines, the Institute is conducting research on
problems affecting cultures and societies as the result of the increasing
number of international, cross-cultural interactions that are occurring among
states, governmental and inter-governmental organizations, networks and
groups. Such interactions may be affected by the differing social and cultural
perceptions of the participants in the interactions. The *results* of the interactions (for example, a new trade agreement, a new treaty, a new policy for the
conduct of business by multinational corporations) may have an impact on
the participants' cultures and societies and on the cultures and societies of
other nations.

The report describes some recent work carried out by an Institute research
team on the international uses of *language*, particularly the English language,
when it is used for purposes of international communication.

All references to persons in the text are to members of the team, except those
persons whose names are followed by an asterisk. Background information
about team members is given in the Appendix.

Language for Mediation

As part of a study on cross-cultural interaction (Bickley, 1981), I have noted that "linguism" can exacerbate tensions among individuals in the same language community, or in different language communities within a single country, or it can create an intercultural problem which affects individuals from different countries. Languages and varieties of languages, however, can provide a "bridge to understanding" when they are used to *mediate* between persons from the same or from different communities. I use *mediate* here to stand for the efforts made by individuals to accommodate each other through language (both verbal and non-verbal) so that there is a satisfactory social encounter, and, therefore, mutual communication, that is, meaning is not being conveyed only in one direction.

Persons from the same culture and language community may use their common language and observe linguistic and cultural "etiquette" for purposes of mediation, for example, expressions such as "I see" are used to fill gaps in a conversation to provide reassurance that the listener is participating actively in that conversation. Marshall* (1968) and Phillips* (1965) have given examples of how a common language is used for mediation in an African language community and in Thai society, and Geertz* (1960), in a well-known example, has noted that in Javanese society the participants in a speech event will use linguistic etiquette to protect their "inward feelings from external disturbances" (that is, they use language in order to *mediate* with each other).

Other devices are used by people for mediating purposes in situations in which they are involved with persons from their own cultures and language communities, with persons from cultures and language communities other than their own and with persons from *countries* other than their own. These include code-switching and code-mixing and also *correction*, a term used by Neustupny* (1978) to mean all kinds of treatment of language, whether by language planners, institutions or individuals. In a recent paper, Bjorn Jernudd and Elizabeth Thuan (in preparation) assert that each individual speaker possesses language as a communicative resource. This resource, they believe, consists of the ability to generate expression, and the knowledge and ability to use expression appropriately in different contexts. Every speaker has available to him a range of language resources "directed to the anticipation of communicative trouble, the detection and circumvention of such trouble as it occurs and to the repair of trouble that has occurred." Jernudd and Thuan include this capability of speakers within the meaning of language correction and consider the role of correction, conventionalization and accommodation, in speaking and in the speech situation, as ways of "easing the burden of communication and as factors contributing to successful interaction."

Persons involved in a communicative act who do not possess a common language may use a third language, for example, an international language such as English, if neither understands the language of the other, or, if they are unable to speak to each other in a third language, then the mediating services of a third person may be required. This third person, the mediator, must be familiar not only with the languages of the two participants, but must also possess some knowledge of each other's cultures.

Mediators include such persons as managers of touring entertainers and sportsmen, business agents for foreign companies, tourist guides, foreign consultants, translators and interpreters. The role of interpreter is particularly taxing since, as Richard Brislin (1980) has observed, intercultural communication difficulties include not only linguistic factors but also factors such as non-verbal behavior, different bases for making contributions about others, and biases stemming from the ingroup-outgroup distinction. Examples of non-verbal behavior that can cause miscommunication in cross-cultural interactions are *facial expressions* ("display rules" in various culture determine when the facial expressions can be used and when it is more desirable to "mask" the expression), *personal distance* (the amount of space two people keep between each other and which varies from culture to culture) and *body movements* (much can be learned about the emotions of another person if body movements are interpreted correctly). "Attribution" is concerned with how and why people make judgments about themselves and others. In cross-cultural encounters, there may be many mistakes in attribution since people bring very different experiences to the encounters. The ingroup-outgroup distinction refers to the relations between members of various groups (for example, sub-cultures) within a given country.

Brislin suggests that intepreters could expand their roles and achieve greater satisfaction, productivity and professional pride if they would incorporate these additional facets of intercultural communication into their work.

Communicative Competence

I have indicated earlier that choice of language or language variety may depend on whether or not the language is required to mediate between persons from different ethnic or national backgrounds. It may also depend upon the user's attitude towards the language selected, on the influence on him of the language community of which he is a part and on factors such as the "communicative competence" of the participants. Competence may be improved if inadequacies may be accurately evaluated and corrective measures taken. Richard Via (1976, 1981) and Anjum Haque (unpublished manuscript) have suggested ways in which the appropriate use of drama techniques may satisfy the three main demands that communicative competence places upon the foreign learner and the teacher, that is, the development of the individual, appropriateness of use of language within a social context and the necessity of acculturation. Mayuri Sukwiwat and John Fieg (forthcoming) are attempting to pinpoint precisely the various problems that Thai speakers have in communicating in English with non-Thais. They are now working on a handbook that will suggest ways to improve such communication. The novel feature of this handbook is that it is an attempt to categorize systematically problems of syntax, semantics, verbal behavior, and cultural differences—and relate these four areas to specific functions such as expressing gratitude, compliments, disagreement, etc. They have reordered and synthesized the functional categories proposed by D. A. Wilkins (1976) and have selected 20 categories which seem to embrace the most frequent and important areas of human interaction. To gather data for the various problem areas, Sukwiwat and Fieg have administered a 150-item communicative capability test to 148 Thais in the United States and in Thailand and have conducted in-depth interviews with a number of Thais in Honolulu.

Sukwiwat and Fieg are also seeking answers to such questions as: Is there a different pattern of rhetoric in different cultures? If there is, how can people coming from different cultures be prepared to understand and operate effectively in the American patterns of debate, discussion, analysis, and exposition? Are the 20 function categories deemed crucial for interactions between members of any two language groups? To what extent can (and should) a teacher insist that his/her students conform to the sociolinguistic norms of the native speakers? (Fieg, 1980)

Language Policy and "Language Planning"

The discussion so far has been concerned with choices of language and language varieties made by individuals and with their ability to mediate successfully with each other. Particular languages and varieties of languages may also be selected deliberately for purposes of mediation *intra*nationally (within one country) and *inter*nationally (between or among countries). Planning for language use within a nation is, of course, normally carried out in the interests of the nation state, although all national language programs have consequences for international relations. Selma Sonntag (in preparation[i]) has derived from a review of language policy literature a list of sixty-six factors or variables influencing language policy on the national level. The list is divided into the six general areas political, economic, social, educational, linguistic and organizational. In a separate study (in preparation[ii]), Sonntag has reviewed a number of linguistic and sociolinguistic surveys, concentrating on those that identify language needs, language demands and language supply on the national level.

After analysing reports of surveys such as those made by Melvin Fox* (1979) on U.S. international language policy, specifically English language policy (which uses profusely the terms "needs" and "demand" without defining these terms concretely); by John Spencer* (1963) on "Third World" linguistic demands and by Fishman, Cooper and Conrad* (editors, 1977) on the "Spread of English," Sonntag concludes that the two greatest gaps that need to be filled in sociolinguistic survey literature are: (1) the gap between implicit assumptions and explicit statements of assumptions and (2) the gap between how language needs, language demands and language supply are usually identified and assessed and how they *should* be identified and assessed in order to draw a realistic picture.

Lack of constraint in the use of the word *need* is also noted by Bjorn Jernudd in a 1979 review of Harrison, Prator and Tucker's English-Language Policy Survey of Jordan (1975). Jernudd points out that there is a "need" corresponding to every discrepancy between the ideal we aspire to and the present as we perceive it, *unless* criteria of evaluation, of constraint, are specified. Observing that these criteria are not provided by the authors of the survey, Jernudd expresses the hope that his comments will stimulate discussion about the practical application of the study of the role of English in Jordan.

> "Such discussion should aim at uncovering ways in which one can approach directly the question of *alternative functions in the future* for English and other languages in a nation that seeks the aid of sociolinguistics to inform decisions about education. It should also aim at discovering ways in which sociolinguistics can contribute to evaluating these alternative futures in terms of constraints. and relative costs and benefits." (1979, pp. 84 and 88).

In addition to those language policies that are planned by nation states for their own national purposes, such policies are also formulated and implemented by inter-governmental organizations and by non-governmental organizations, such as multinational corporations, to ensure satisfactory multidirectional communication among the national representatives and staff members of those organizations. For example, many of the organizations listed in the *Yearbook of International Organizations* have adopted English as an official working language and as the language or one of the languages they believe will best serve such a purpose. Among such organizations are Amnesty International, the Inter-Parliamentary Union, the Asian Development Bank, the Asian Industrial Development Council, the Pacific Basic Economic Council, the Association of International Libraries, the Association of Secretaries General of Parliaments, the International Passenger Ship Association, the Atlantic Treaty Association and the Baltic and International Maritime Conference.

English as an International Language

In the years that have passed since the end of the War of 1939–1945, different roles have been created for the English language largely as the result of the expansion of international travel and advances in communication technology, combined with policy decisions made by nations and governmental, inter-governmental and non-governmental organizations. In Burma, for example, Burmese has replaced English as the medium of instruction at colleges, institutes and universities and English is now a compulsory foreign language in the education system, being taught at all levels from Standard V in the high school and above. In Malaysia, English no longer has the status of an official language although it is the major "second" language of the Malaysian educational system.

Although English is classified by "outsiders" as a foreign language in Burma and a "second" language in Malaysia, the terms "English as a Foreign Language" and "English as a Second Language" are no longer adequate to describe the functions of the language in those and in other countries. In a number of articles (1976, 1979) and in an edited volume to be published in 1981, Larry Smith has proposed "English as an International Language" as a blanket term to cover all the functions of English as it is actually used in different parts of the world. James Baxter (1980) has pointed out that the English as a Foreign Language (EFL) and English as a Second Language (ESL) characterizations share the common elements of predicting who the interactors in a situation will be. In an EFL situation, one interactor (whether face-to-face or at a distance) is always a native speaker. In an ESL situation, the interactors may be non-native speakers of the same national membership (for example, India), or in a similar intranational setting, one interactor may be a native speaker. Baxter notes that when a person has the ability to speak (or write) English internationally, there is no preconceived idea as to who the potential interactor(s) in a communicative exchange will be, whether in terms of nationality, linguistic background or cultural background. In a teaching situation he believes that whereas in EFL and ESL specific varieties of English and specific cultures can be dealt with, the goal in the teaching of English as an International Language cannot be knowledge of the details of a given variety of culture, or even numbers of these. Students must somehow be prepared to operate with English in unknown situations which are characterized by variation in linguistic and cultural behaviour. Central, therefore, to the EIL approach are the realities of diversity and adaptation. As an introduction to some comments on "interactive listening," Baxter notes that full recognition is given to the fact that other languages function internationally but that English is used most frequently in international settings. English as an International Language is conceptually distinct from Basic English. It also differs from such languages as Esperanto in not being an artificial language and in not asserting the belief that the widespread adoption of a common tongue will lead to global harmony. It places in the forefront the reality that from a sharing of commonalities such as grammar, lexis and phonology, communication does not automatically flow. EIL provides, says Baxter, the means of perceiving that enhanced world communication is possible only through recognizing all those areas of behaviour which are *not* shared across national or cultural lines. Furthermore, Baxter points out that EIL is not an instance of English for Special Purposes (ESP), for example, a specific linguistic corpus for diplomats or international businesspersons.

In sum, English as an International Language situations are frequent and can be classified in terms of the interactors engaged in those situations. They include situations in which native speakers of English who come from differing national and cultural backgrounds are involved. English does not "belong" to any one group of people. The use of English is always culture-bound, but the English language is not bound to any specific culture or political system.

World Maps, Survey of Teaching Institutions and Intelligibility Study

As part of the continuing study of the actual uses of English as an International Language, Bjorn Jernudd and William Shaw (in preparation) sought measures which differentiate between speech communities in regard to the amount of use of international languages, and which are practical in terms of the time it takes to assemble the information. They compiled tables and maps on the uses of English and a number of other languages of wider communication in the world's nations—the importance of any one language, they claim, is really only apparent if compared with the use of another—as *official* languages, in *daily newspapers*, in domestic and overseas *broadcasting* and in *university instruction*.

Larry Smith, Donald Campbell, Anjum Haque and Peansiri Vongvipanond (in preparation) are attempting to classify language problems identified by language teaching institutions which prepare people to use an international language in international settings. They have designed a survey instrument which is being used in the United States as well as in a number of countries of Asia, including Hong Kong, India, Japan, Malaysia, Pakistan, the Philippines, the People's Republic of China, Taiwan, Sri Lanka, Singapore and Thailand. The survey consists of a questionnaire and an additional interview and it is based on two working hypotheses—(1) that in a communicative act in which the participants vary in cultural, social and ethnic backgrounds, as well as in language competence, problems are certain to occur which may affect the success of the communication, and (2) that these problems are the effects of certain causal factors which must be recognized if a solution to the problems is to be found. The subjects being studied in the survey are institutions which offer teaching programs for the use of English in international settings. Analysis of the responses to the written questionnaire is now underway and interviews have begun.

Larry Smith and John Bisazza (in preparation) have begun to test the intelligibility of different varieties of English for different speakers of English in the United States and in countries in Asia and the Pacific. They have defined intelligibility for their purposes as the understanding of the communicative signal which depends primarily on linguistic rather than cultural or contextual factors. In this study, the variation in syntax among varieties of English is held constant while the phonological/phonetic factors are allowed to vary. Forms of the same listening comprehension test are read by speakers with different accents to test listening comprehension. The test will be given in nine countries and the results obtained will be discussed in terms of current work on the intelligibility of different varieties of English.

Language in International Business

Use of the term "English as an International Language" by the Culture Learning Institute is based on the premise that the English language and the culture of the user of the language are linked. James Baxter has observed that a similar link is found in business, with culture being both the culture of the environment as well as the sub-culture of the business world. Baxter (1980) has prepared a short bibliography on "Language in International Business" which mainly includes items describing the use of English in the international business context. Many of the entries discuss the relation of English-language use to cross-cultural and business training and the connections between English and the uses of other languages which function internationally.

The bibliography does not focus exclusively on one function of the English language but rather, in a context within which the use of English in international business may be explored, on topics such as management training, cross-cultural training, business communications, adaptation to new environments—and problems encountered in the use of English.

Language Problems in International Organizations

Although not solely concerned with the English language, a recent study by Bjorn Jernudd and Elizabeth Thuan (in preparation) provides some insights into the difficulties faced by international businesses and international organizations that must legislate for language use.

In 1979–1980, Jernudd and Thuan set themselves the following questions: How are problems of language interaction in international settings dealt with? What language correction systems (support systems for solving language problems) have been established to assist use of international languages in international settings? How is knowledge about ways of dealing with problems of interaction in international settings created, shared and used? How might international settings be organized and managed to avoid or to deal more effectively with language problems? How do individual correction needs motivate organized correction of language use?

With these questions in mind, they chose to begin their study in the area of fisheries because fisheries, although not strictly a single organization, is international in scope, uses a number of languages, is geographically diverse and economically important, and requires co-operative networks at many levels. Within the field of fisheries, they focused on fish-naming since that aspect of fisheries is of interest to all those involved in fishing and is not as dependent on technological development as other aspects of the fishing industry. Furthermore, they note that fish-naming is an internationally organized, historically well-founded, and geographically widely dispersed activity.

Jernudd and Thuan point out that language is the most crucial social and cultural factor that influences co-operation in the international linkages that are necessary to ensure that the ocean continues to provide the world with fish for food. Their study is therefore an attempt to determine which problems of language use arise in interaction in the field of fisheries, particularly such interactions as are internationally connected; how such problems are dealt with by individuals and organizations, what are considered effective means of resolution, and what other social and cultural factors are related to and affected by problems of international language use and means of resolving language problems.

In 1979 and 1980, Jernudd and Thuan interviewed a number of persons in Hawaii and Australia in the fisheries field and also distributed a letter questionnaire to a selection of national standardization agencies, language planning agencies, U.S. government organizations and agencies concerned with fisheries and a number of U.S. profit or non-profit, private organizations that service fisheries.

They note that language problems directly affect cultural, social, political and economic realities in the fisheries industry and beyond. Different fish-names and differing fish-naming systems and also different terminologies for fisheries products, create barriers between fishermen, consumers, processors, scientists, information experts, government officials, language experts and other individuals and also between inter-governmental organizations, governmental agencies, profit enterprise, and professional associations. Different communities that use the language or languages seek different solutions, whether knowingly or unknowingly, to the same or equivalent language problems, for example, the differential standardization of preferred common names in languages such as English. The consequences of differential usages in international languages and languages of wider communication are likely to be severe for data banks and term banks that serve translators.

Jernudd and Thuan believe that, although some new ways of thinking about the problems of fish-naming have been proposed, lack of appreciation of cultural and linguistic factors and insufficient information about current usage limit their applicability and chances for success. They conclude that an increased research effort could lead to better understanding of language intervention by international agencies in international languages and languages of wider communication and particularly in regard to terminology and translation.

Such research may be carried out more effectively within a framework for the study of international languages in international organizations. A paper by John Brownell describing such a framework is now in preparation. The framework maps out a multidisciplinary approach to a number of individual studies. Brownell is also gathering data related to the language problems of international research and development performing organizations. The latter is a specific exercise to obtain data in one aspect of the framework.

Sociolinguistic Futures

In 1979, the International Federation of Semi-Official and International Institutions (Fédèration des institutions internationales) sponsored a seminar on the use of languages in organizations and meetings. The Preface to the seminar report notes that it was convened to

> encourage a free exchange of views among those who are confronted daily with the problems of language that are posed by the very fact that an international organization necessarily transcends national, cultural, and linguistic borders. And yet it is manifestly impossible for any international organization to work in all the languages normally used by all its members. Moreover, any single language used in different geographical and cultural regions is likely to exhibit widely varying characteristics, expressions, styles, accents and rhythms . . . one might say, in brief, that languages are essential tools of international relations and international comprehension, and therefore of the process in which international organizations are fundamentally engaged . . .

As this statement implies, and as the study by Jernudd and Thuan referred to above establishes, the difficulties that face members of international organizations in communicating effectively across national and cultural boundaries are very real, despite the increased use of English as an international language. It is possible that the problem could be alleviated to some extent if a satisfactory model could be constructed capable of forecasting the present and future demands for an international language such as English and for other international languages. Preliminary work in the designing of such a model at the Culture Learning Institute has been reported by Selma Sonntag (in preparation[iii]). In her paper, she describes, analyzes and evaluates seven sociolinguistic "scenarios", each of which finds a prominent niche for English. These scenarios are as described in Ali Mazrui's* *A World Federation of Cultures* (1976), and in publications by Robert Textor (forthcoming), Lester Brown, Jacob Ornstein, Burnham Beckwith, Joshua Fishman and Sonntag herself.

Sonntag notes that, although English is listed in each scenario, Jacob Ornstein (1977) and Burnham Beckwith (1978) emphasize the spread of an artificial language, Lester Brown (1972) and Sonntag emphasize the spread of English, Mazrui (1976) and Fishman (1973) emphasize the spread of international languages including English, and the ASEAN group and Fishman emphasize the growth of non-international languages. All seven of the scenario writers conclude that a growth of language communication in the international sphere is likely and none suggest that the future world will be characterized by a retreat to isolation and autarchy. Sonntag concludes that this similarity could be the basis of departure for future research on constructing a model capable of forecasting present and future demands for an international language and for a number of international languages. Certainly, the English language seems to be assured of its place.

REFERENCES

(Not including members of the Culture Learning Institute)

BECKWITH, B., "The Next Five Centuries: A Prospective History Based on Current Trends," in *The Futurist*, Vol. II, No. 5, pp. 85–89, 1968 (Review Article).

BROWN, L., *World Without Borders*, Random House, New York (1972).

FISHMAN, J. "Will Foreign Languages Still Be Taught In the Year 2000?" in *Le Français dans le Monde*, No. 100, October-November, Paris, 1973.

FISHMAN, J., COOPER, R., ROSENBAUM, Y., "English Around the World," (Chapter Two) in Fishman, J., Cooper, R., and Conrad, W. (eds.), *The Spread of English*, Newbury House, Rowley, Massachusetts, 1977.

FOX, M. J., "U.S. International English Language Policy," in *Language in Public Life*, J. E. Alatis and G. R. Tucker (eds.), Georgetown University Round Table of Languages and Linguistics, Georgetown University Press, pp. 8–22, Washington, D.C., 1979.

GEERTZ, C., *The Religion of Java*, Free Press of Glencoe, New York, 1960.

MARSHALL, L., Extract:"Sharing, Talking and Giving: Relief of Social Tensions Among Kung Bushmen," in *Readings in the Sociology of Language*, J. Fishman (ed.), Mouton, Paris, 1968.

MAZRUI, A., *A World Federation of Cultures: An African Perspective*, The Free Press, New York, 1976.

NEUSTUPNY, J., *Post-Structural Approaches to Language: Language Theory in a Japanese Context*, University of Tokyo Press, Tokyo, 1978.

ORNSTEIN, J., "Reflections of a Linguist on the Unending Quest for a World Language—Negative, Positive and Prospects," *Review of Applied Linguistics*, Vol. 38, pp. 3–27, Belgium, 1977.

PHILLIPS, H. P., *Thai Peasant Personality*, Berkeley: University of California Press, 1965.

SPENCER, J., "Language and Independence," in *Language in Africa*, pp. 25–39, Cambridge, University Press, Cambridge, 1963.

TEXTOR, R., "Alternative Futures for ASEAN: An Educational Perspective," Stanford University, forthcoming.

WILKINS, D., *Notional Syllabuses*, Oxford University Press, Oxford, 1976.

NOTES ON THE CULTURE LEARNING INSTITUTE RESEARCH TEAM

JAMES BAXTER was a professional associate with the Culture Learning Institute from October, 1979 to July, 1980. He is a member of the staff of the Stanford University for Intercultural Communication.

> *References*: "Interactive Listening" *TESOL Reporter*, 1980.
> "Language in International Business: An annotated bibliography," Culture Learning Institute, 1980.

VERNER BICKLEY has been Director of the Culture Learning Institute since 1971. He is also President of the Hawaii Branch of the English-Speaking Union of the United States.

> *References*: "Language as the Bridge," in *Cultures in Contact: Studies in Cross-Cultural Interaction*, S. Bochner (ed.) Pergamon Press, Oxford, 1981.

RICHARD BRISLIN is a research associate with the Institute. He is the author of numerous books and articles on cross-cultural interaction and was coordinator of work done at the Institute which led to the Handbook of Cross-Cultural Psychology (1980).

> *References*: "Expanding the Role of the Interpreter to Include Multiple Facets of Intercultural Communication," in *International Journal of Intercultural Relations*, Vol. 4, pp. 137–148, Pergamon Press, 1980.

JOHN BISAZZA is the recipient of an East-West Center scholarship and is a doctoral candidate in linguistics at the University of Hawaii. He has lived and worked in Japan.

> *Reference*: "Intelligibility study of varieties of English" (publication in preparation with Larry Smith)

JOHN BROWNELL is a research associate in the Institute. His publications include *Japan's Second Language*, *Curriculum and the Disciplines of Knowledge* and *A Directory of Selected Resources for the Study of English in Japan*.

> *Reference*: "Framework for the Study of International Languages in International Organizations" (in preparation)

DONALD CAMPBELL has an East-West Center scholarship to study for a Master's Degree in English as a Second Language at the University of Hawaii. He served as a Peace Corps Volunteer in Thailand before coming to Hawaii.

> *Reference*: "Survey of institutions teaching English for International Communication" (publication in preparation with Larry Smith).

JOHN FIEG has been a professional associate at the Institute since January, 1980. He received a Master's Degree in English as a Second Language from the University of Hawaii in 1979.

References: A Handbook of Thai-English Communicative Capability (with Mayuri
Sukwiwat—publication in preparation).
"Language Standards and Native-Speaker Norms—An Historical Analysis"
(Culture Learning Institute Working Paper, 1980)

ANJUM HAQUE has an East-West Center scholarship to study for a Master's Degree in English as a Second Language at the University of Hawaii. She is on leave from the University of Baluchistan, Pakistan, where she is a member of the academic staff.

Reference: "Drama and Communicative Competence" (unpublished manuscript).

BJORN JERNUDD is a research associate with the Institute. He has been Senior Lecturer in Linguistics at Monash University, Senior Fellow in the East-West Center and Project Specialist, Ford Foundation, Cairo Field Office.

References: "Evaluation in Language Planning—What Has the Last Decade Accomplished?" in *Progress in Language Planning*, J. Cobarrubias and J. A. Fishman (eds.), Mouton, Paris (in press).
"Language Problems in the Fisheries Industry—A Report" (publication in preparation with Elizabeth Thuan)
Review of "English Language Policy Survey of Jordan: A Case Study of Language Planning," W. Harrison, C. Prator, R. Tucker (eds.) in *Language in Society*, **8**: 1, Cambridge University Press, Cambridge, 1979.
World Maps of English and Other Languages of Wider Communication (in preparation with Willard Shaw).
"To Err is Human: Control of Language Through Correction I" (in preparation with Elizabeth Thuan).

WILLARD SHAW received an East-West Center scholarship to study for a Master's Degree in English as a Second Language at the University of Hawaii. He was awarded the degree in 1977. From 1978 to 1979 he was a professional associate in the Institute. Before joining the East-West Center he served in the Peace Corps as Fisheries Extension Agent in Nepal from 1967 to 1972.

Reference: *World Maps of Uses of English and Other Languages of Wider Communication* (with Bjorn Jernudd—in preparation)

SELMA SONNTAG was a professional associate in the Institute from January to September 1980. She is an M.A. candidate in Political Science at the Univerity of Washington in Seattle, specializing in language planning and policy formulation and implementation.

References: (i) "Factors in Language Policy" (publication in preparation)
(ii) "Sociolinguistic Surveys" (publication in preparation)
(iii) "Sociolinguistic Futures" (publication in preparation)

LARRY SMITH is a research associate in the Institute.

References: (ed.) *English for Cross-Cultural Communication*, Macmillan and Co., London, March, 1981.
"Intelligibility study of varieties of English," (publication in preparation with John Bisazza)
"Surveys of institutions teaching English for International Communications," (publication in preparation with Donald Campbell, Anjum Haque, and Peansiri Vongvipanond).

"English as an International, Auxiliary Language," *RELC Journal*, **7** (2), 38–53, Singapore, 1976.
"English for Cross-Cultural Communication: The Question of Intelligibility," in *TESOL Quarterly*, **13** (3), 371–380, 1979.

MAYURI SUKWIWAT has been a research fellow at the Institute since 1977. She was formerly the Director of the Central Institute of English Language, Bangkok, Thailand, and Secretary of the National Committee for the Co-ordination of English Instruction.

Reference: "A Handbook of Thai-English Communicative Capability" (publication in preparation with John Fieg)

ELIZABETH THUAN was a Senior Teaching Fellow in the Department of Linguistics at Monash University and a member of the faculty of the State College of Victoria at Clayton, Australia. She was a professional associate in the Culture Learning Institute from October 1979 to September 1980.

References: "Language Problems in the Fisheries Industry—A Report" (publication in preparation with Bjorn Jernudd)
"To Err is Human: Control of Language Through Correction I" (in preparation with Bjorn Jernudd)

RICHARD VIA is an educational specialist with the Institute. For twenty-three years he was an actor, stage manager and director in the professional theatre.

References: *English in Three Acts*, University Press of Hawaii, Honolulu, 1976.
"Via Drama: An Answer to the EIIL Problem" in L. Smith (ed.) *English for Cross-Cultural Communication*, Macmillan and Co., London, 1981.

PEANSIRI VONGVIPANOND has an East-West Center scholarship and is a doctoral candidate in linguistics at the University of Hawaii. After completing her doctorate she will be returning to Thailand where she is a member of the staff of Chulalongkorn University, Bangkok.

Reference: "Survey of Institutions Teaching English for International Communication" (publication in preparation with Larry Smith, Donald Campbell and Anjum Haque).

Appendix

**ENGLISH AS AN INTERNATIONAL LANGUAGE:
INTELLIGIBILITY vs. INTERPRETABILITY.
NOTES ON A THEME**

CHRISTOPHER N. CANDLIN

University of Lancaster

I. *Intelligibility vs Interpretability*

Intelligibility of world English *text* vs interpretability of world English *communication*.

An international version of a national (and a linguistic) problem.

Misinterpretation due not only to surface textual disturbances, but critically to:

  (a) social-psychological factors of *attitude* (affective & cognitive) (cf. *Giles & St. Clair* 1979)
  (b) sociolinguistic factors of *role, status & social knowledge* (cf. *Labov* 1972; *Levinson* 1979; *Labov & Fanshel* 1977)
  (c) psycholinguistic factors of *interpretative "potential"* (cf. *Clark & Clark* 1977; *Slobin* 1979)

Interpretability as a "richer" (and inherently more complex) problem than intelligibility.

Examples:
1. "When do you plan t'come home"
  (a) Request for information
  (b) Request for action
  (c) Request for help
  (d) Challenge to mother's performance of her role as head of house
  (e) Admission of inability to cope with obligations
                                        (*Labov & Fanshel* 1977)

---

2. "From the speaker's point of view the problem is: 'Given that I want to change the state of the hearer in such a way, how do I frame my utterance in order to make that outcome most likely?' From the hearer's point of view, it is 'Given that the speaker said so-and-so, what is the most likely reason for his saying so-and-so' "

(Leech 1979)

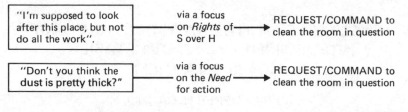

(Labov, 1972)

3. M: I said within myself "You know, you don't matter so what are you talking to me for?" And the other one was I felt.
   F: What was the sentence "You don't matter?"
   M: I felt I didn't talk directly to you.
   F: You said some words like, "You don't matter."
   M: Yes. You don't matter.
   F: Say this again.
   M: You don't matter at all.
   F: Say it again.
   M: You don't matter at all.
   F: Say it to a few more people.
   M: You don't, you don't really matter . . .

(cited in *Levinson* 1979)

II. *Factors in assessing English for International Communication*

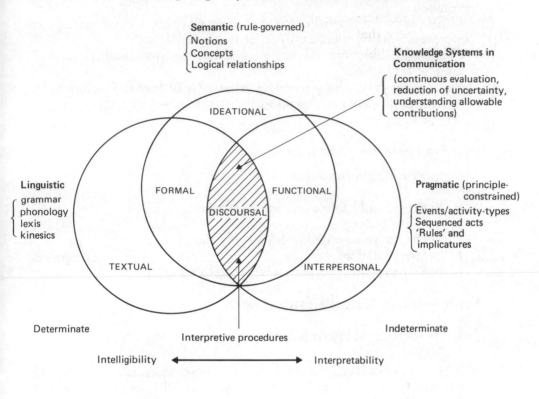

Semantic (rule-governed)
⎧ Notions
⎨ Concepts
⎩ Logical relationships

Knowledge Systems in Communication
⎧ (continuous evaluation,
⎪ reduction of uncertainty,
⎨ understanding allowable
⎩ contributions)

IDEATIONAL

Linguistic
⎧ grammar
⎨ phonology
⎪ lexis
⎩ kinesics

FORMAL   FUNCTIONAL

DISCOURSAL

Pragmatic (principle-constrained)
⎧ Events/activity-types
⎨ Sequenced acts
⎪ 'Rules' and
⎩ implicatures

TEXTUAL   INTERPERSONAL

Determinate   Indeterminate

Interpretive procedures

Intelligibility ⟷ Interpretability

III. *Problems facing Interpretability*

1. Textual (Linguistic)
2. Ideational (Semantic)   } 4. Discoursal "capacity"
3. Interpersonal (Pragmatic)   (Psycholinguistic)

Questions:
Which of 1–4 above, and which within 1–4 above, can we assert to be universal across Englishes?
If any are universal, are they thus unproblematic for interpretability?
If any are not, where are the likely sources of misinterpretation?

IV. *Some Research worth undertaking*
   (*inter alia*)

(a) Are "rules" for interpreting utterances socially and culturally specific? Do they vary across languages, across Englishes?

(b) Are there universal activity-types? Do special activity-types require different kinds of inferencing/interpreting? Are "similar" activity-types coded differently in different Englishes?

(c) What effect do so-called "restricted" codes/languages have on interpretability?

(d) Within particular Englishes are there key textual factors which impede interpretability by speakers of other Englishes?

(e) What social functions do universal acts (say, questioning) play in different Englishes?

(f) What social-psychological values attach to different Englishes, to other English speakers? To non-English speakers?

etc., etc., etc.

V. *Some Practice worth Preaching*

1 { (a) Provide information on culture/society/context
    (b) Provide information on textual structure } of Englishes

2 { (a) Heighten awareness of inferencing and interpretation
    (b) Provide particular purposes for interpreting } of Englishes

3 { (a) Acknowledge alternatives from 2
    (b) Tolerate misinterpretation } across Englishes

VI. "But how many kinds of sentence are there? Say, assertion, question and command? There are *countless* kinds: countless different kinds of use of what we call 'symbols, words, sentences'. And this multiplicity is not something fixed, given once and for all; but new types of language, new language games, as we may say, come into existence, and others become obsolete and get forgotten . . ."

(*Wittgenstein*, quoted in *Levinson* 1979)

BIBLIOGRAPHY

CANDLIN, C. N. "Discoursal patterning and the equalising of interpretive opportunity," in Smith, L. (ed.) *English for Cross-Cultural Communication*, Macmillan, London.

CLARK, H. and CLARK, E. *Psychology & Language: an Introduction to Psycholinguistics*. Harcourt, Brace, 1977.

GILES, H. and ST. CLAIR, R. *Language and Social Psychology*. Blackwell, 1979.

LABOV, W. *Sociolinguistic Patterns*. University of Pennsylvania Press, 1972.

LABOV, W. and FANSHEL, D. *Therapeutic Discourse*. Academic Press, 1977.

LEVINSON, S. "Activity Types and Language," in *Linguistics 17*, 1979.

LEECH, G. N. "Pragmatics and conversational Rhetoric", mimeo. University of Lancaster, 1979.

SLOBIN, D. *Psycholinguistics*. Scott, Foresman, 1979.